# A MOTHER

## Constance Congdon

based on
*VASSA ZHELEZNOVA*
by Maxim Gorky
translated by Tanya Chebotarev

**BROADWAY PLAY PUBLISHING INC**
New York
www.broadwayplaypublishing.com
info@broadwayplaypublishing.com

A MOTHER

© Copyright 2004 Constance Congdon

Cover art compliments of American Conservatory Theater

First printing: June 2004

I S B N: 978-0-88145-243-3

Book design: Marie Donovan

Word processing: Microsoft Word

Typographic controls: Xerox Ventura Publisher 2.0 P E

Typeface: Palatino

Printed and bound in the U S A

A MOTHER was first produced by the American
Conservatory Theater in San Francisco, opening on
19 May 2004. The cast and creative contributors:

| | |
|---|---|
| LIUDMILA | René Augesen |
| LIPA | Jeri Lynn Cohen |
| VASSA | Olympia Dukakis |
| PAVEL | John Keating |
| PROKHOR | Tom Mardirosian |
| ANNA | Marcia Pizzo |
| SEMYON | Reg Rogers |
| NATALYA | Margaret Schenck |
| MIKHAIL | Louis Zorich |

| | |
|---|---|
| *Director* | Carey Perloff |
| *Scenery* | Ralph Funicello |
| *Costumes* | Beaver Bauer |
| *Lighting* | James F Ingalls |
| *Sound* | Garth Hemphill |
| *Singing coach* | Peter Maleitzke |
| *Dramaturg* | Paul Walsh |
| *Casting* | Meryl Lind Shaw |
| *Assistant director* | Steven Anthony Jones |

# CHARACTERS & SETTING

VASSA PETROVNA ZHELEZNOVA, *wife of Zakhar*
PAVEL, *her child*
ANNA, *her child*
SEMYON, *her child*
NATALYA, SEMYON's *wife*
LIUDMILA, PAVEL's *wife and* MIKHAIL's *daughter*
PROKHOR ZHELEZNOV, *Zakhar's brother and* VASSA's
  *brother-in-law*
MIKHAIL VASSILYEV, *the manager*
LIPA, *the maid*

*The play tales place in 1909 in a small provincial town on the Volga.*

# ACT ONE

*(Early hours of the morning.* VASSA ZHELEZNOVA *sits at her desk, a large piece of furniture covered with papers in piles, each pile weighted down with a ceramic tile. She's been up all night and looks tired. From upstairs,* LIPA *comes down, carrying some dirty linen. She exits. Then* MIKHAIL *comes down and crosses to* VASSA.)

VASSA: How is he?

MIKHAIL: Bad.

VASSA: How bad?

MIKHAIL: I'm not a doctor.

VASSA: How could Zakhar leave me like this?

MIKHAIL: He's had a stroke.

VASSA: That's no excuse! It's irresponsible! What about the business? He's up there, silent as a rock, staring at the ceiling.

MIKHAIL: He's dying, Vassa Petrovna.

VASSA: Yes. And I haven't found a single piece of paper—absolutely nothing to protect what you and I have spent our lifetimes building up. Are you certain he didn't leave something at the factory?

MIKHAIL: Nothing. I looked and looked. He never left anything at the factory, anyway. Not even an order. He wouldn't. There's no reason to—they're all illiterate. *(Beat)* What can we do?

VASSA: We have to make a will ourselves. And get him to sign it.

(LIPA *re-enters with some letters.*)

MIKHAIL: He can't hold a pen.

VASSA: Don't sneak up on me like that!!

LIPA: The mail is here.

VASSA: Tell me when you're entering.

(VASSA *grabs the letters, goes through them.* LIPA *keeps talking, oblivious or used to the abuse.*)

LIPA: Poor Zakharushka. He was sick all night. And he can't even ask for help. Except from God, of course.

VASSA: Still no telegram from Anna! Her father's at death's door and where is she? Why doesn't she come?

LIPA: He just stares up at me, his little eyes just blinking away. Like a baby.

VASSA: Lipa, go away!

(LIPA *exits*)

MIKHAIL: Anna will come. I'm sure of it. But what's the rush? It's not as if he knows any of us are here.

VASSA: Oh, he knows. I'm sure his brain is turning and turning.

MIKHAIL: It's just that I thought she gave up whatever inheritance she would have had when she married that…person Zakhar Ivan'ich didn't approve of.

VASSA: He was a drunk and Zakhar knew it! Not one of my children has made a good choice in marriage. *(Beat)* So your daughter is married to my son! But who could call that a good match? She doesn't love him! Who could? Only a mother, only a mother could love him.

MIKHAIL: I'm a little worried about you confiding in Anna and not me. Because I'm resting all my hopes on you, Vassa Petrovna.

VASSA: You don't think you're going to be taken care of? You don't think you can trust me? You're the only one I trust, Mikhail. That's always been true. And Liudmila—I trust her. I do. She's your daughter. And I've raised her to be like me.

MIKHAIL: There's no one like you, Vassa Petrovna.

VASSA: But people don't confide in me—I don't know why. Anna was the one. They've always told her everything.

MIKHAIL: You mean the boys.

VASSA: I've spent thirty years wondering what to do with him. Nothing seems to work.

MIKHAIL: They can't do anything if we—YOU—write the will a certain way—

VASSA: "Sole, unrestricted ownership"—to me. That's the phrase we need. No magic lawyer words around it—that just muddles everything up.

MIKHAIL: And then we'll be safe. Am I right? What Semyon and Pavel want to do won't matter anymore. They'll have no legal basis for—

VASSA: Do you think they'll keep quiet? They'll scream to high heaven. But I'm supposed to be thankful and respectful when the lawyers step in and inform me that since there is no will, I will get the widow's share. And then I'm supposed to be quiet and accept my fate as another indigent old lady living on the kindnesses of my sons and their wives. And you—what will happen to you? You will be little father-in law in a cold back room somewhere, god help you.

MIKHAIL: Yes. God help me.

VASSA: Mikhail. Stop being afraid. And stop questioning my decisions. I need Anna to help me control my sons. I do not want anyone to even suspect that we have any controversy here. Controversy is very bad for business. Under this roof, well, we have our problems. But as far as the rest of the world goes, we're a happy family with a strong, healthy company. We heat their homes with peat and we make tiles for their roofs. They should trust us. Trust is very important for business.

MIKHAIL: We're forging this will to keep the trust of our customers.

VASSA: That's right.

MIKHAIL: Of course, Vassa Petrovna.

VASSA: Zheleznov and Sons! That's what it's called, this business that you and I have spent our lives running. It's not Zheleznov and Wife or Zheleznov and—whatever we would call you.

MIKHAIL: Partner, I would hope. Or—

VASSA: Don't push it too hard, Mikhail.

MIKHAIL: Manager is fine. That's how the customers know me. We want everything to run smoothly after…

VASSA: Yes. After. Not that I'm wishing Zakhar be taken before his time. He is my husband.

MIKHAIL: Yes. And a fine…employer.

VASSA: He started this business! Let's not forget that! All of this—from his head.

(Beat)

MIKHAIL: And our backs.

VASSA: And it could all be gone in a few days unless we make a will. Oh, I've had an interesting night, Mischa. With the books. And the truth. (She makes

*certain no one can see them and gives him a piece of paper.)*
Here's a draft of the will. It's clear and the language
is proper. Now copy it out—it shouldn't be in my
handwriting. Go back there, where no one can see you.

*(MIKHAIL tucks himself behind some piles of papers to
continue writing; VASSA rings for LIPA. LIPA enters.)*

VASSA: Where were you?

LIPA: The samovar is coming in.

VASSA: Are my children up? Because I don't want to be
disturbed.

LIPA: Semyon is up because his wife went to sit with
Zakharushka.

VASSA: Stop calling him "Zakharushka."

LIPA: He's just so sweet, that husband of yours.

VASSA: Everyone's sweet when they're paralyzed and
can't speak. You're so sentimental, Olympiada. I don't
know how you've survived this long. Tell Semyon not
to bother me. And Pavel—where is Pavel? Probably
still in bed.

LIPA: No, Vassa Petrovna.

VASSA: Really?

LIPA: He never went to bed. He was up all night.

VASSA: So was I. I didn't see him.

LIPA: He was moving back and forth all night—
bedroom, front hall, bedroom, front hall, bedroom,
front hall—

VASSA: Stop!
Just tell me—is he sick again?
LIPA: No, Vassa Petrovna.

VASSA: Lipa! Tell me!

LIPA: His wife didn't come home last night.

(MIKHAIL *hears this. For* VASSA *it's a flash of recognition of disaster, and then a way to fix it.*)

VASSA: She spent the night at her father's house.

LIPA: Except her hair is mussed and her clothes are all wrinkled like they weren't hung up. And she has on clothes she wore yesterday when she has some nice dresses at her father's house.

VASSA: Oh, you're just full of details, aren't you?

LIPA: I'm just doing what you want me to do which is to tell you everything.

VASSA: She spent the night at her father's house! You enjoy telling me things like this? Things that will upset me?

LIPA: But Vassa Petrovna, I'm just doing what you want me to do.

VASSA: Get out of here and make the beds, as if nothing happened. Because nothing did happen!

LIPA: Yes, Vassa Petrovna. (*Exits*)

VASSA: What kind of parent are you? Your daughter just leaves for the night? With god knows who?

MIKHAIL: I can't control her! What am I supposed to do!

VASSA: This will finish Pavel. This will kill my boy.

MIKHAIL: What about my daughter? If they find out in the village, she'll never live it down. She'll be a prisoner of this house. If Pavel keeps her. What if he divorces her? Where will she go? And what will happen to me, if the boys inherit and I lose everything!?

VASSA: Pull yourself together. Look at me! I'm not panicking , so you don't, either. I was up all night with all this. The figures are terrible, worse than last month—and last month was worse than the month before. But there's no hysteria here. We've had quite enough hysteria. The whole country may be falling apart, but we're not. Give me what you've written. *(She reads it.)* Perfect. Good, Mikhailo. We need three witnesses to sign this document.

MIKHAIL: We'll have to pay them.

VASSA: I know that! Of course! But don't let them take you.

MIKHAIL: Don't worry. Antip Mukhoedov owes us money for all those tiles for his silo and Ryzhev hasn't paid anything on his fuel bill for months.

VASSA: They're desperate. That's good. Who else?

MIKHAIL: I'll go through the books—

VASSA: Not enough time. Grab the next visitor who can read and who's not a family member—someone we can trust to sign and shut up about it. Pay him whatever he wants. Don't bargain. We'll just have to buy him outright.

MIKHAIL: I understand. I'll do exactly as you say, Vassa Petrovna.

VASSA: Mikhail, don't worry. My boy will keep your Liudmila. He loves her. Oh, I'm exhausted.

MIKHAIL: Have you slept at all?

VASSA: What? Do I look bad?

MIKHAIL: No. Never, Vassa Petrovna.

*(PAVEL enters, sobbing.)*

PAVEL: Mother! Have you heard? My wife is a whore!! And look who's here? My honorable father-in-law! Where is your daughter, huh? Oh, that's right! She spent the night at your house because she missed her Daddy and that smokey stove and broken-down chair,

I'm sure. Oh, I'm sure that's where she was all night! Mommy, Mommy, I am so miserable! My heart has been cut open!

MIKHAIL: Pavel Zakharovich, by the law of the church, my daughter is your wife! She's yours—not mine!

VASSA: Mikhail. Mischa—just go, go!

(MIKHAIL *exits.*)

PAVEL: Run, little doggie! *(Barks after him)*

VASSA: Pavel, get a hold of yourself! Such a display!

PAVEL: Mother! I am completely humiliated. It's unbearable.

VASSA: I told you she's no match for you. Why couldn't you have married a quiet, simple girl?

PAVEL: "Simple?" You mean, mentally deficient? Or how about malformed? Like me! Pavel Zakarovich is a freak, so let's get him a freak for a wife!

VASSA: You're not a freak, Pavel. But the way you carry on sometimes…

PAVEL: Oh yes. "It's not your affliction that embarrasses me, my son. It's your behavior."

VASSA: If you want someone to feel sorry for you, you're living in the wrong house!

PAVEL: What other house do I have?

VASSA: Oh, just stop it! Sit down and have some tea.

PAVEL: Tea? Tea! Oh, that will fix everything! The Russian solution for all that ails you! Drink this! Eat this! And for godsake, don't cry!!

VASSA: Oh God.

PAVEL: Mama, please. If I could just get out of here for a while! Give me some money! I'll go to town just for a little while…

VASSA: Pavel, your father is sick, very sick. Have you been up there to see him? Just lying there, staring at the ceiling? Your *father*. And then you go into town? "Why, look at that! It's Zakhar Zheleznov's oldest son living it up while his father is dying and their business is failing."

PAVEL: The business is failing?

VASSA: The business is fine. Don't worry about the business.

PAVEL: You always do this! No matter what the tragedy is, it always comes back to the business. That's all you ever talk about is the business! My life is over! My life was over before it ever began!

VASSA: Go over there and calm down. I haven't even had time for *my* tea.

(PAVEL *exits to some place unseen but still nearby.* NATALYA *enters.*)

NATALYA: Good morning, Mother-In-Law.

VASSA: You're always first for tea when there are cakes, Natalya. Where's my son? Where's Semyon?

NATALYA: I don't know. We missed each other.

(PAVEL *begins to cry.*)

NATALYA: I sat up with Father-In-Law because he was so sick in the night. Is someone…crying in here?

VASSA: Pavel! Shame on you! Hysterical woman!

NATALYA: Oh, poor boy. Lipa, get him some water!

VASSA: Pavel! I should have smothered you in your crib!!

NATALYA: Pavushka. It's all right.

VASSA: See what you make me say to you!

PAVEL: Don't touch me! Either of you! You are disgusted with me! My wife goes out on a spree!!

(PAVEL *exits.* LIPA *enters, looks at* VASSA *for instruction.)*

VASSA: Get some water, Olympiada!

(LIPA *exits to get the water.* NATALYA *runs after* PAVEL. VASSA *catches her.)*

VASSA: You are married to my *other* son—*Semyon.* Did you forget?

NATALYA: Pavushka, wait!

(NATALYA *exits after* PAVEL. MIKHAIL *enters.)*

MIKHAIL: I need to see you. Alone.

VASSA: What's wrong?

(LIPA *returns with water.)*

VASSA: Lipa, go away!

(LIPA *exits with the water.)*

MIKHAIL: My daughter went away with Prokhor.

VASSA: No! Where?

MIKHAIL: To the farmstead.

VASSA: Oh, you mean last night! That's where she was last night! Oh my god, my heart stopped. I thought she had gone away somewhere forever.

MIKHAIL: She might as well have. That horrible man took my daughter to the farmstead and…. That man who has been flirting with her ever since she married your son. Sometimes I think Prokhor wanted her to marry Pavel, just so he could have her under this roof—that way his lechery could run wild.

VASSA: *"Run wild"?* This is my house, Mikhail!

MIKHAIL: I'm sorry. I just meant he could have opportunities. Where he could wear her down. Wear down her defenses. This man. And people think he's kind. That he has "a conscience." "Conscience" and "kindness." I have seen them at work. They're like sand in a machine. And philosophy! He's good at that! This idea. That idea. It's all a big game to him. A quote from some opera or some play! As if the boys in the factory even know what he's talking about. Give me as much as I'm worth, nothing more!! No jokes! No pats on the back! And keep your slimy hands off my daughter's future!

VASSA: But he helped us through some lean times. We would have gone under without his money.

MIKHAIL: I know. I know.

VASSA: We can't get distracted. Have you gotten the signatures?

MIKHAIL: I'm going now. It'll all be done by lunch.

VASSA: Father Yegor is coming for his daily visit at lunchtime! And then he goes up to pray over Zakhar with Natalya. Need I say that Zakhar must be alive while that happens?

MIKHAIL: He's resting quietly. His breathing is good. For now. But who knows how he's going to be in the next moment? This is all very hard. It's been a very hard day. It's not even breakfast yet.

(MIKHAIL *exits and* VASSA *shouts after him.*)

VASSA: You want an easy life? Starting when? *(To herself)*

(LIPA *enters.*)

VASSA: What do you want?

LIPA: I heard you screaming. I thought it was for me.

VASSA: Well, it wasn't for once. I need to freshen up. And change my dress. There's a lot more left of this hellish day. Clean up in here, but don't touch anything on the desk!

(VASSA *exits.* LIPA *crosses to the samovar and starts to clean up but is overcome with sorrow and anxiety for everything that's going on in the house. She slips down until she's kneeling by the samovar. Then she crosses herself, three quick times from right to left—Russian Orthodox—and prays to an icon of Mary and Jesus.*)

LIPA: Holy Mother, preserve and pardon your servants and their ways.

(SEMYON *enters.*)

LIPA: Semyon! I'm scared. Bad things are happening here.

SEMYON: Is there tea?

LIPA: Yes, I will get you some. It's so awful. I've been waiting to tell you. No one went to bed last night.

SEMYON: —and cakes?

LIPA: Your mother was up all night working. Your Natalya was up helping me, taking care of Zakharushka—I mean, your father. Prokhor was gone all night. Pavel didn't go to bed.

SEMYON: Wait. Pavel didn't go to bed?

LIPA: No.

SEMYON: Lipa, there's someone missing from this list. *Mrs* Pavel. Liudmila. Did she go to bed?

LIPA: She didn't spend the night at home.

SEMYON: She didn't spend the night at home because…I don't understand.

LIPA: She spent the night with your uncle.

SEMYON: Oh my god!

LIPA: He took her to the farmstead. Pavel knows she spent the night with someone but he doesn't know—

SEMYON: (*Revolted*) Uncle Prokhor, you dog, you!

SEMYON: He's been working on that for years! And he finally made it! I can just see the look on Pavel's face. His wife "slept" with Uncle Prokhor—as if she got a moment to sleep all night long!

PROKHOR: *(Entering)* Do you know what that cripple of a nephew, that scheming, little Rigoletto of a man did?

SEMYON: No.

PROKHOR: He let a cat loose in with my prize pigeons! One of the boys came to get me and there I'm standing looking at a skobar and this beautiful black, dead. Dead. No more. They will come no more. *(He quotes Pagliacci: "In my anger, I will crush you under my foot")* *Vo' ne lo sprezzo mio schiacciarti sotto i pi'!!* I can't believe I'm related to that...that *dwarf*! Look at me! Still good-looking and I'm twice his age. *"Ella mi fu rapita! Bella figlia dell'amore."* The tea is cold.

SEMYON: Uncle Prokhor. Did you sleep well?

PROKHOR: And what were you doing with Lipa, you dog? Didn't you finish with her years ago?

SEMYON: I am married to Natalya. She is my *wife*! I am completely loyal to the bonds of marriage.

PROKHOR: You lack the opportunities and the talent, that's all. Look, Senechka, let's not fight. I'm tired. I was up all night you know.

SEMYON: Uncle Prokhor, I know what you did. With Liudmila.

PROKHOR: I said I was *up* all night.

SEMYON: Uncle Prokhor, I can't listen to this.

PROKHOR: Semyon, how can that woman be his wife? She should live in a city! Go to Moscow! Be an actress!

*(LIUDMILA enters. She is dressed in her robe, but looking beautiful. She is tired. There is a silence.)*

LIUDMILA: I see. That obnoxious angel of silence is passing over us. *(Beat)* She'll be gone in a moment, boys. And then you'll have to speak. Because no angel would stay around here.

PROKHOR: Good morning. *"Bella figlia dell'amore."*

LIUDMILA: Signore. Did I say it right?

PROKHOR: Perfecto.

*(LIPA bows as she pours some tea for LIUDMILA.)*

LIUDMILA: *(To LIPA)* I need some milk. Go get me some fresh milk.

*(LIPA exits.)*

LIUDMILA: I don't like spies. *(To PROKHOR) Signore,* you're ogling me.

SEMYON: *Signore?* He looks like a Spaniard.

PROKHOR: When have you ever seen a Spaniard, you blob of dough?

SEMYON: And you were speaking Spanish, too.

PROKHOR: It was Italian.

LIUDMILA: Boys! Be friends. *(To PROKHOR)* I'd like to have some secrets in this house. So try to avoid crowing.

SEMYON: Lipa knows. She told *me.* I think if it weren't for Lipa, none of us would know anything.

PROKHOR: You still have eyes for Lipa.

SEMYON: Uncle Prokhor! Stop it! What if Natalya heard you? She wouldn't understand.

PROKHOR: She doesn't understand much, my dear boy.

SEMYON: Well, that's it! I will not stand here and listen to my Natalya insulted!

PROKHOR: Relax, Senechka. You know we all love your little wife, your little mama, your matriushka doll.

SEMYON: *(Quite touched by the image of his wife)* She does love me...so much—my little matriushka doll.

PROKHOR: So when you unscrew the big Natalya, is there a smaller Natalya inside? And when you unscrew that one, is there an even smaller one, and smaller, and smaller, and smaller, until there's only a teeny, weeny little Natalya? And does she speak in a teeny tiny wittle voice when she calls, "Senechka! Senya! I'm here on the coverlet. Be careful where you sit."

SEMYON: Uncle! You— You— *(Turn on LIUDMILA)* And YOU were laughing!

LIUDMILA: I'm sorry, Semyon.

PROKHOR: Look, Senechka. I'm just feeling my oats a bit. You and Natalya, you come with Liudmila and me and take a troika ride. We've got one coming in about an hour. It'll be fun. And no jokes, I promise.

SEMYON: My Natalya will never approve of the two of you. My Natalya wouldn't get into any carriage with you. And—and—you forget Pavel is my brother.

PROKHOR: And my nephew.

LIUDMILA: And my husband.

*(LIPA enters)*

LIUDMILA: I told you to go!

LIPA: There's a lady—

*(ANNA enters.)*

LIUDMILA: Anna!!

*(LIUDMILA runs and embraces ANNA.)*

ANNA: Liudmila? Is it you?

SEMYON: And me!! Anna, it's me!! Your little Senya! I knew you'd come!

*(They kiss on both cheeks—three times, the Russian way.)*

ANNA: "Little" Senya! You've…grown!

SEMYON: I'm well-fed and happy. I'm married! Wait 'til Mama sees you! You're so different! Lipa! What are you doing standing there? Tell Mama Anna is here!

ANNA: No!

PROKHOR: Anna?

(LIPA *doesn't move.*)

SEMYON: Lipa—go!

LIPA: I can't. She told me not to disturb her. For any reason

PROKHOR: But this is her daughter, you stupid little cow.

ANNA: No. It's all right, Uncle Prokhor.

PROKHOR: "Uncle." No "uncle." Please.

LIUDMILA: Olympiada. Go!

ANNA: No. No. Everyone. Don't tell Mother just yet. I need to—

LIUDMILA: Everyone keep quiet then, all right? And leave us. Please. Just leave us.

PROKHOR: But I just met this sophisticated woman I once knew—

SEMYON: I have to find Natalya. You have to meet my Natalya.

ANNA: Let me rest a moment.

PROKHOR: Lipa! Get our guest some tea!!

LIUDMILA: Everyone!! Get out of here!! Now!! GO!!!

(*They all exit.* LIPA *returns with some tea*)

LIUDMILA: LIPA, GET OUT!! Wait. If Mother finds out Anna is here, I'll know it was you who told her.

(LIPA *exits.*)

ANNA: Giving orders! You're sounding a little too much like….

LIUDMILA: Don't say it. Please. I've had to adapt. It's so good to see you, Anna.

ANNA: You look tired.

LIUDMILA: Thank god you're here. That's all.

ANNA: Why didn't you ever write to me?

PAVEL: *(Enters)* I saw the luggage in the hallway and I knew!

*(PAVEL embraces ANNA. They go into an old pattern from childhood)*

PAVEL: Anna! Save me!

ANNA: So soon, Pavel? But I just got here!

PAVEL: I really need saving this time, Anushka. I am so alone.

LIUDMILA: Pavel, don't start. Please.

PAVEL: *(To* LIUDMILA, *about* ANNA*)* This is my *sister.* *(Lighting the lamps)* We need some light in here. Light means truth. Anna tells the truth. She stood up to Father.

ANNA: It didn't go well, if you remember.

PAVEL: But you got what you wanted. That was the last time I saw you. You've changed. Look at you. You look sad.

*(To* LIUDMILA *who is putting out some of the lamps)*

PAVEL: What are you doing?

LIUDMILA: It's the middle of the day—we don't need lamps. Your mother will hate this.

PAVEL: But I want Anna to really see you, Liudmila. Because you are my *wife.* You are mine.

LIUDMILA: Put those lamps out. It's ridiculous!

PAVEL: No. I won't.

LIUDMILA: Won't you ever just leave me alone?!

PAVEL: No. And I'm lighting more lamps, more and more. All the lamps in the house!

LIUDMILA: Stop it! Freak!

PAVEL: You see, Anna, what kind of satanic creature I am forced to live with—and for the rest of my life.

LIUDMILA: "Forced?" You liar! You *begged* me. You crawled in front of me and begged me!

ANNA: Both of you—be quiet! Do you want Mother to come stomping down here?

LIUDMILA: He tries to hurt me in any way he can. He gave me a Siberian cat for a present. And then he poisoned it.

PAVEL: I didn't poison it. It ate itself to death.

LIUDMILA: Shut up, you—you toad! And get out!!! OUT!!!

PAVEL: I'll be back Anna. I know YOU love me. *(He exits.)*

LIUDMILA: Now you know why I never wrote to you. What would I have said, "Help! I've married Pavel!"

ANNA: Just, "I've married Pavel". I would have known you needed help.

LIUDMILA: I had to marry him, Anna.

ANNA: You got carried away with *passion*? With Pavel?

LIUDMILA: No, not with Pavel. No.

ANNA: Not with Uncle Prokhor.

LIUDMILA: You know about that?

ANNA: Everyone knows.

LIUDMILA: I've had no one for years, Anna. And before there was only this boy I met.

ANNA: What boy?

LIUDMILA: It was during the riots. Everywhere around us there was chaos. And then this lovely boy turns up. He wasn't handsome. His face had pock-marks even. He tried to cover them with a beard. But to me, he was more than handsome. He was beautiful. And then he was gone. He may have been killed. I don't know. I can't think about it.

ANNA: Did Pavel know you were pregnant by this boy?

LIUDMILA: No! Nobody knew but Uncle Prokhor.

ANNA: Uncle Prokhor! Of all people-why?

LIUDMILA: He helped me-get rid of it. I couldn't go to anybody else. How could I go to your mother? I know she's fond of me, but I wasn't a member of the family then. I was alone, Anna. Prokhor is a man of the world and I know he's had many adventures. So I asked him for help and he got it for me. But, of course, by then I was already married to Pavel.

ANNA: Couldn't you have carried the child and saved yourself a lot of grief? Pavel would have thought it was his?

LIUDMILA: It would have been born four months early.

ANNA: But babies are early sometimes.

LIUDMILA: It would have looked like a full-term baby.

ANNA: That's what swaddling clothes are for.

LIUDMILA: All right! Pavel and I hadn't…consummated the marriage. I—I can't stand him, Anna! And it's made me bitter and cruel. I don't recognize myself sometimes. *(Beat)* I was a better person when I was with that boy—and happy. He was gentle.

(PROKHOR *sings offstage.*)

ANNA: How about Uncle Prokhor? Is he *gentle*?

LIUDMILA: He's nice to me. And he really did help me when I was desperate. When someone does you a favor, you return it—that's how civilized people act. Right, Anna?

ANNA: How would I know how civilized people act? I grew up here.

SEMYON: Oh! You're still in here. I can't find Natalya.

(ANNA *grabs* SEMYON.)

ANNA: Semyon, don't go around shouting—Mother will know something is up. And I just can't face her yet.

SEMYON: I'll be quiet. Don't worry. (*He exits, whispering "Natalya" in the loudest sotto voce one can do.*)

ANNA: Oh god. We may be cruel in this family, but we're not stupid. Where did he come from?

LIUDMILA: You think we're cruel? I can't tell any more. Anna—why are you here? Really.

ANNA: What do you mean? Father—

LIUDMILA: You hate him. He threw you out of the house.

ANNA: You know, time makes things…. (*She can't bring herself to lie about this.*) I need money.

LIUDMILA: But you're not getting anything. Everybody knows that.

ANNA: I might contest that.

LIUDMILA: Oh my. Would you like a drink? I know where the vodka is.

ANNA: Mother would smell it on my breath.

(LIPA *crosses the stage.*)

LIUDMILA: Enough with my life. I'm sick of thinking about it. What about your life? Your husband? Your children.

ANNA: You mean the children who lived.

LIUDMILA: I'm so sorry none of us came.

ANNA: It seems such a long time ago now.

LIUDMILA: *(Out at the garden)* Pavel!! Get out of there!! He's in the garden! He's stepping on the flowers!! Pavel!!

ANNA: Flowers? Since when has Mother planted flowers?

LIUDMILA: Pavel!! Get out of there!!

ANNA: Mother hasn't gotten senile or anything, has she?

LIUDMILA: Clumsy idiot!!

LIUDMILA: He's gone. He just does that because Mama and I planted it together. I hope he didn't do any damage. See? Those are fruit trees. She bought me a book on pruning and I got good at it.

ANNA: She bought you a BOOK?

LIUDMILA: You should see her out there ripping out the weeds. She loves the garden, Anna.

ANNA: Loves? Of course, vegetation has very simple needs. It doesn't talk back. And it certainly never asks for money.

LIUDMILA: Are you actually going to ask Mother for money?

ANNA: I have to! I can't stand to live with my husband for another day. I want to come home. With my children. Mother has to help me. I have to get her to help me. I'm desperate, Liuda.

NATALYA: *(Crosses upstage doors)* Senia! Senia!

LIUDMILA: My advice? Don't come begging, then. Make her come to you. Didn't she just stand there when your father threw you out of the house? That's what I heard. She owes you—at least an apology. And when, you know, you lost the baby, she didn't come. Well, none of us did anything. We didn't find out until months later.

ANNA: The only reason I even wrote to her about it was out of spite.

LIUDMILA: Then why are you afraid of her?

ANNA: Because I need her.

PAVEL: *(Enters with a bouquet of flowers he picked in the garden)* Ludochka, look what I picked for you. I'm sorry. Please. Just look at me?

LIUDMILA: Anna, I have to get out of here. Don't let Mama know I've seen you. She'll think we're conspiring or something. *(She exits quickly.)*

PAVEL: She ran away. Can't even look at me? So, I suffer. And I make sure she suffers as well. *(Beat)* Anushka, help me, for God's sake! I'll give you whatever you want—money? Do you want money? I'll give it to you! After Father finally dies. Yes! I'll give you everything…everything! I mean it! *(Beat)* I really mean this, Anna. My word on it.

*(LIPA crosses stage. PAVEL waits for her to exit.)*

PAVEL: I'll sign a paper.
Look at me. I'm calm now. Do we have a deal?

*(PAVEL insists on a handshake between them.)*

ANNA: All right. What can I do to help you?

PAVEL: You got married for love. You have it in your heart, so give it to her. Teach her how to love, and then teach her how to love me.

ANNA: Oh, Pavel. I can't do that. No one can. Ask me to do something I can do.

PAVEL: I kneel by her bed: "Liudmila, Liudochka, nobody can love you as much as I do." I whisper all night long until morning. "I have no one else to live for, only for you."

ANNA: Oh no, someone is coming. If it's Mother—. Pavel, listen to me—I just arrived a moment ago. You got that?

PAVEL: Of course. You just this moment sat down. I made you sit down—that's it.

ANNA: All right.

NATALYA: *(Enters)* Pasha, Mother is wanting to see you. Quickly! She's angry.

PAVEL: Something new! Mother is angry!

ANNA: Did she say anything about me?

NATALYA: I don't know who you are. *(To PAVEL)* Someone said you hit one of the office boys.

PAVEL: How can anyone expect me to be kind when I'm treated with so much cruelty every moment of the day! *(He exits.)*

ANNA: Poor Pavel

NATALYA: That's what I say, but no one listens to me.

*(ANNA knows she has to snap out of her fear of her mother and try to be normal. And NATALYA is expecting an introduction because that's "proper".)*

ANNA: I'm Anna.

NATALYA: Pleased to meet you, I'm sure. I'm Natalya and my Semyon wants me and you to become friends.

ANNA: I just got here less than a minute ago and I need to go see my mother.

NATALYA: You can't see her now. I know because I tried. She's changing her clothes. She was up all night and looked rumpled. And then she has to rake Pavel over the coals, so she'll be busy for a while. Besides, she knows you're here. Your coach driver told the boy who brings the milk and he told the cook. And then the cook asked me to ask your mother if she could make a big lunch since you've arrived. Cook consults me because I am second mistress of the house. So I knocked on your mother's door and she told me to go away. So then I got piece of paper and wrote it all down in a note and slipped it underneath your mother's door and knocked to tell her it was there. And then I went back a few minutes later to see if she had gotten the note and it was gone but your mother must have heard me outside the door because she shouted that I was to get Pavel since I was so fond of him and tell him that she found out he hit one of the office boys and now she was very angry and demanded to see Pavel right now. I probably look rumpled, too, since I was up all night, just like her, but with Father-in-Law. But as soon as I see my Semyon, I'll be happy and won't need to rest anymore.

ANNA: How nice for you.

NATALYA: He is my little Senya. He makes me smile and laugh and so on. And soon he will make me a mistress. Of my own household. I shouldn't have told you that.

ANNA: Oh, why.

NATALYA: Because Mother-in-law shouldn't know.

ANNA: My mother.

NATALYA: Yes.

ANNA: Why shouldn't she know?

NATALYA: Well, it doesn't matter because you're not going to inherit anyway. But it would upset Mother-in-law because she wants us all to stay here and keep the business so she can't know that we're going to take our share and *go live in town*. And I can't say anymore. But Senya and I need to be safe because around here it's ominous.

ANNA: Oh, you just mean sad. Because my father is dying? He's an old man.

NATALYA: No, Senya definitely said "ominous." I can't explain it quite. But we need to live in fortified towns where there would be a lot of police and even army. Around here and probably everywhere, there are fewer and fewer just normal people, Sister-in-Law. Everybody has started thinking a lot. And then all these strange Wanderers everywhere. One came to our house, just recently, and tried to convince us that every act of work is a sin, and we don't need to do anything! I lie there thinking at night—what would happen if nobody worked ever again? These things worry me. And we want to be safe. But Mother-in-law would try to stop us if she knew.

(PROKHOR *enters.*)

PROKHOR: Where's Rigoletto? Oh, his champion, his nanny is here. Well, Natalya, you might tell your little pet Pasha, your little maimed pony, that I know it was he who removed the ladder up to my pigeon loft WHILE I WAS UP THERE, thinking I wouldn't notice and FALL TO MY DEATH. And I plan to torment him until he confesses and apologizes!!!

NATALYA: (*To* PROKHOR) You care more about your pigeons than you own family! And if you continue to be mean to Pavel, you may drive him to violence! Yes, he may hit you someday! And that is breaking a Commandment.

PROKHOR: Advice and an Indictment from Balaam's ass.

NATALYA: How dare you use such language in my presence!

PROKHOR: It's a story in the Bible, a book I thought you had some familiarity with. Perhaps you'd popped over to the kitchen for a bite of something when your papa read that part. The *ass* that belonged to Balaam was, in fact, a four-legged beast of burden. That is what the word "ass" means. For example, if, say, *you* had a lot of weight to carry, you would need a very large ass. Luckily, God has provided.

NATALYA: I'm not certain what you're saying, but I know it's insulting. And I know my Semyon wouldn't like it. *(She exits.)*

PROKHOR: *(To* ANNA*)* How do you like her so far? She could be one of my breeding pigeons, but with the personality of a snake.

*(*PROKHOR *produces a cigarette for* ANNA. *She can't resist that. He lights it for her.)*

PROKHOR: Cigarette? Aren't you worried about Vassa finding you down here? Without you seeking her out and doing the proper obeisance? Or—are you playing a game by making her come to you? You need to decide and then use it to your best advantage.

ANNA: Oh, she knows I'm down here. She always knows everything. Games don't work with her—I should know that by now. She always wins. Besides, she's changing her clothes. It's the one thing she never rushes. She always wants to look good. Has she aged much?

PROKHOR: Have I?

*(*SEMYON *enters and whispers.)*

SEMYON: Mother's coming.

(VASSA *enters, looking fresh, with a different dress. She ignores* ANNA *totally.*)

VASSA: Semyon! Go to the factory! It's still a work day.

SEMYON: Anna's here, Mama!

VASSA: Semyon!

(SEMYON *gets up and exits.*)

ANNA: Hello, Mama.

VASSA: Why is it that I'm the only one around here who seems to work.

(*During the following exchange,* ANNA *crosses to* VASSA, *but* VASSA *isn't receptive*)

PROKHOR: (*Shouting after* SEMYON) Oh, and while you're "working," don't be too smart, like you did the last time she left you at the helm. Took your mother a week to straighten out the mess!

SEMYON: (*Beyond words*) You are a—bad man!

PROKHOR: Oh, a palpable hit!

(SEMYON *exits*)

PROKHOR: (*To* VASSA—*a soldier's greeting to a senior officer—he salutes.*) Good morning, Sir.

(*No reply from* VASSA—*he continues as if she did speak.*)

PROKHOR: Your son just stabbed me in the heart, but I will be able to fulfill my duties, Sir.

ANNA: Mama—

VASSA: You smell of cigarettes. Go up and see your father.

(ANNA *exits.*)

PROKHOR: Boom! She clears the room.

VASSA: Now who is responsible for upsetting Natalya?

PROKHOR: She's upset? How can you tell? I find her face totally inexpressive. Like a cow.

VASSA: She was standing outside my door, her face so white it looked blue, pulling little tassels out of her shawl.

PROKHOR: She's excitable and flighty. So strange for one with her shape.

VASSA: I know it was you. It's always you.

PROKHOR: But not with Pavel. He's the one who always starts it. He's trying to kill me now! And he murdered my pigeons!

VASSA: Prokhor Ivan'ich, you are my husband's brother and I know you are not a stupid or evil man.

PROKHOR: But I'm bad, evidently. You heard your son, Vassonka. I'm a "bad man."

VASSA: That's Semyon—always stating the obvious. Now, listen to me. I know you have the capacity to understand what an embarrassment your behavior is for the entire household. And at a time when our business looks bad in front of everyone we know.

PROKHOR: Ah, this lecture. Well, I have heard it from your husband, many times over the years, when he was still able to speak, of course. Being my brother, he felt it was his duty to remind me that I was being an embarrassment. *Except*, of course, except when he needed my money. So I'll say to you what I've always said to him—it's too late to teach me. And now, it's actually true. I'm an old dog and you know what they say about them.

VASSA: Liudmila is very young. She's barely more than a girl. She needs to have a real life.

PROKHOR: A "real life"? Like her marriage to Pavel?? Well, my hat's off to you, Vassa Petrovna— you were certainly thinking about Liudmila's needs when you arranged all that. Luckily, I know quite a bit about young women and what they "need."

VASSA: But Pavel is your own nephew!

PROKHOR: Yes, and let him know that if he doesn't stop killing my pigeons, I will—

VASSA: Your *pigeons*? You're worried about your pigeons? And what will you do if he kills all of them?

PROKHOR: I will rip his ears off!

VASSA: You would attack a boy—

PROKHOR: He's a man! He's thirty-four years old!

VASSA: —over some birds?

PROKHOR: They are *my* birds.

VASSA: And *she* is his wife!!

(PROKHOR *doesn't answer. He's too angry. He turns his back to take some medicine from a small bottle he takes from his pocket*)

VASSA: What are you doing? You turn your back on me?

PROKHOR: I'm trying to restrain my anger, Vassa Petrovna.

VASSA: Don't bother. It's clear you have no loyalty to this family.

PROKHOR: (*Turning back around*) Loyalty? My soon-to-be-late brother, with your help, nearly ruined me, utterly and completely. Thirty thousand of mine gone, as if you both inhaled it. "Invested," you said. And now the business is in trouble again? Boom! This wallet is closed. And I want my thirty thousand rubles? I don't owe this family anything. In fact, the family owes me! Me!

VASSA: Then, dear brother-in-law, there will be a terrible fight.

PROKHOR: With whom?

VASSA: With your nephews.

PROKHOR: And not you, Vassa Petrovna Zheleznova? You're the scary one.

VASSA: I only care about the business. I want the business to survive.

PROKHOR: Then don't threaten me. Or I'll stab it in the heart. For real.

(PROKHOR *exits.* VASSA *sits and tries to calm down.* ANNA *enters, looks at her mother for a moment before she is noticed.*)

ANNA: Mama… Father is very bad. He looks terrible. I don't think he knew me.

VASSA: You look so sophisticated.

ANNA: I know how to dress.

VASSA: You learned it from me. But you've been to better dressmakers. So how is your husband?

ANNA: Promoted to Lieutenant-Colonel.

VASSA: Does he still drink?

ANNA: He's an officer. That's what they do.
Yes, more than ever.

VASSA: And my grandchildren.

ANNA: All right. They're all right.

VASSA: But your firstborn died.

ANNA: I survived it. It was a difficult pregnancy. And I was alone, completely and absolutely alone.

VASSA: The great passion you had for this man is completely gone, isn't it? But, oh, how it boiled at the time. It welled up and took you over. You wouldn't listen to anyone.

ANNA: And now, he's sick. And has been for a long time.

VASSA: And yet, my daughter, you have managed to have more children, even with a sick husband who's drunk most of the time.

ANNA: You are a smart woman, Mama. You're perceptive.

VASSA: I think you have been the smart woman. You made a new generation, however you did it.

ANNA: But I can't raise them on a military pension and I'm afraid I will be a widow very soon.

VASSA: Your father gave you your inheritance.

ANNA: Threw it at me! And it was a fraction of what I would get!

VASSA: You signed a paper.

ANNA: It was witnessed by Mikhail, your employee. A case could be made—

VASSA: Are you threatening me, Anna. Do you know who you're dealing with?

ANNA: Oh yes. And that's why I'm not begging.

VASSA: You're not?

ANNA: I'm bargaining.

VASSA: With what? What do you have that I could possibly want?

ANNA: My complete loyalty. My total honesty…from this moment on. And some information you might want to know.

VASSA: I'll consider it. If it's new information.

ANNA: I know what's at stake, Mama. Does Father have a Will and Testament?

VASSA: I don't know.

ANNA: You? Don't know?

VASSA: I don't know.
I haven't found one.

ANNA: So, legally, my brothers will inherit.

VASSA: Yes, and I'll get the widow's share. A pittance.

ANNA: And what will happen to the business, then? You have got to be worried about what they will do with the money.

VASSA: Oh, yes.

(SEMYON *enters loudly looking for* NATALYA *and exits.*)

ANNA: Well, my brothers have always confided in me.

VASSA: That's true.

ANNA: Actually, they've already told me a couple of things.

VASSA: What? What have they told you?

ANNA: I won't tell you, until you look me in the eye and promise me that my children and I will be taken care of.

VASSA: Do you trust me?

ANNA: I have no choice.

VASSA: All right, I agree.

ANNA: You agree to…

VASSA: …consider taking care of you and your children.

ANNA: You'll *consider* it?

VASSA: That's all I can do until I know how much of the estate I'll have. There may be nothing if your brothers get control of it. No matter how many ways you divide nothing, it is still nothing. I may have to come to live with you on your military pension.

*(Beat)*

ANNA: According to Semyon's wife, he's planning to move to town.

VASSA: And what is he going to do there? Sit in the square and pretend to be intelligent? His money will be gone in six months!

ANNA: She said something about being "mistress of the house." Her own house.

VASSA: Oh god.

ANNA: You must have expected this, Mama. Children grow up and leave home and start their own lives.

VASSA: Like you?

*(ANNA is silent.)*

VASSA: We have a much bigger problem right now. Your Uncle Prokhor may take his money out of the business. Yes. And whose work made the business grow? Mine and Zakhar's. What has that indulgent, pompous fool ever done? Chased every woman in sight and invested in theaters. And now what does he need money for? He's alone. And he lives here! For free!

ANNA: And what would happen if he took his money out?

VASSA: The business would collapse!

ANNA: Even with Uncle Prokhor's money, are we going bankrupt now?

VASSA: Over my dead body. But after your father dies—it's another story.

ANNA: Did he ever think about me? What was going to happen to me?

VASSA: If you had made a good marriage that would have been good for the company, you would have received the full share Zakhar set aside for you. Your father wasn't a cruel man, he was ill.

ANNA: "Ill?" Crazy!

VASSA: His illness made him crazy. And now, he's had a stroke. We made a life for all of you that was better than anything we had or dreamed of having. And what bothers me, what burns inside me is knowing that no one realizes what we went through. All this— *(About the house, clothing)* —inconceivable when I was a child. But it could go away so quickly and I would be in poverty again. As an old lady. You will still have your pension, even though it won't be enough. But my sons? And their wives? How would they survive? Out there. I shudder to think. Can you see? I save myself and them. But I lose them, too. They'd become my enemies.

ANNA: You're worried about losing the love of Semyon and Pavel?

VASSA: You don't think they love me? They do! Like lion cubs love their mother. They take me for granted. And they fear me. But to have them hate me, Anna. After I was long dead, they might realize that the reason they aren't destitute is because I kept them from squandering their inheritance. But the years in between, Anna—the loneliness and the fear—terrible. Terrible.

ANNA: I didn't think you cared what we felt about you or what you felt about us.

VASSA: So you think love is *feelings*? Love is food, shelter, clothing, heat, clean water. That's love. And the

person that gives you that loves you. What good are
feelings when you're starving?

ANNA: Except for loneliness, Mother.

VASSA: Yes. That's it. That's my weakness. I admit it.
That's the woman in me.

ANNA: And I didn't think you were afraid of anything.

VASSA: Then you weren't paying attention. Listen—
unless people are beholden to you in some way,
you can't survive. Never be dependent on charity or
peoples' "good will".

ANNA: Like I'm dependent on yours. Now.

VASSA: That's right.

ANNA: But it's for my children that I'm asking. I would
do anything to see that my children survive. And I
want them to love me. I want them to feel love for me.
And I would be terribly lonely if they didn't.

VASSA: It's the mother's curse. Luckily, you have it
much worse than I do.

(LIPA *enters.*)

LIPA: Father Yegor is here.

VASSA: *(To* ANNA*)* Go freshen up. I'm glad you're here.

(ANNA *exits.*)

VASSA: *(To* LIPA*)* Who is upstairs with Zakhar right
now?

LIPA: Mikhail.

VASSA: Go tell him the priest is here.

LIPA: He knows. *(But she doesn't leave.)*

VASSA: What?

LIPA: I have to tell you something I forgot to tell you
and I don't want you to be angry.

(VASSA *is silent.*)

LIPA: Prokhor Ivan'ich had a visitor from town last night.

VASSA: Before he went to the farmstead with Liudmila? He was a busy man last night.

LIPA: It was Evgenii Mironych.

VASSA: He's a lawyer! What did they talk about?

LIPA: I couldn't hear.

VASSA: What? You hear everything!

LIPA: They locked the door.

VASSA: But there's an air-hole in the stove!

LIPA: They were too quiet. I couldn't hear. Honestly, Vassa Petrovna, I couldn't hear a word!

VASSA: After all I've done for you! I've protected you!

LIPA: I couldn't hear them!! I tried.

VASSA: Have you forgotten the crime you committed?

LIPA: Vassa Petrovna, please—I can't think about it.

VASSA: Well, you need to think about it. It is only because of me you're not in prison or hanged by now!

LIPA: Can I just go to a convent? Send me to a convent! I would rather be cloistered for the rest of my life, then live here and be constantly tormented!

VASSA: Convent!? Send you to a monastery! You can clean up after all the crows, with their long beards and smelly robes. Wouldn't they like a girl like you? Those monks, the dross of every family, the village idiots, the cripples.

LIPA: Cripples? Then send your own son to a monastery! God forgive me.

VASSA: What?

LIPA: I was speaking to God.

VASSA: No, you weren't.

LIPA: I'm sorry, Vassa Petrovna. I didn't mean it about Pavel Zakar'ich going to a monastery.

VASSA: Of course, you meant it. And don't think I haven't thought of it. Hundreds of times. But it's a prison without bars. I'd be sending my son to prison.

LIPA: Send both of us away, then—Pavel Zakar'ich and me. We're the two unhappiest people in this house!

VASSA: Oh, I doubt that. Now, wipe your face. And remember, any place other than here and you'd be lost. Now go. Go.

(LIPA *exits, passing* MIKHAIL *who enters with a tiny plate of Russian gnoshes.*)

VASSA: Why aren't you with Zakhar?

MIKHAIL: I was just up there. He's fine.
I mean, he's…breathing all right.

VASSA: But, what if—? Where is the priest?!

MIKHAIL: He's eating—what else? The cook sent up this perog for you. There will be a big lunch later. I told her: "Dammit! I'm not a servant!"

VASSA: Watch your language in my presence, Mikhail Vassil'ich! I am still mistress here!

MIKHAIL: I'm sorry. Everyone is making jokes about Liudmila and Prokhor.

VASSA: Forget about it. They are all fools and idiots. We have another problem. Prokhor saw a lawyer last night.

MIKHAIL: I know. Lipa told me.

VASSA: She told you before she told me?

MIKHAIL: I made her tell you. She was afraid you'd be angry because she didn't report it immediately.

VASSA: She's forgotten to be scared of us. She's talking back to me, more and more. Standing up for herself.

MIKHAIL: Standing up for herself? Forgotten how to be scared? She murdered her own infant.

VASSA: It's very dangerous if she's not afraid. She could tell anyone where the child came from.

MIKHAIL: But nobody could prove anything. It's not as if the infant came with a trademark. And there are no remains. The mother is under this roof, but unstable. And the father? We don't know who he was. He's gone away. And we never knew. And she has these fantasies….

VASSA: But the gossip. The gossip would have a life of its own.

MIKHAIL: That would be a death blow. No one would buy our tiles. They'd only buy peat because they have to have it every day.

VASSA: You talk to her. Men are better at that. You scare the Hell out of her. Be very, very stern and tell her that she would have nothing, nothing if she left here. *Nothing*. And then pet her and make her feel loved. And needed. Need is a good one. Women fall for that all the time. They like to be loved. But they liked to be needed above all other things. It's a curse from God.

MIKHAIL: But what do we do about Prokhor?

VASSA: It's so unfair. What can we do about him?

MIKHAIL: His heart is bad. Very bad. He could go at any minute.

VASSA: Oh, he'll outlive both of us. If only for spite.

MIKHAIL: He takes medicine for his heart. And it's a strong dose, too.

VASSA: Oh?

MIKHAIL: He trusts Lipa to administer his dosage when he has an attack. She could… forget. Or drop it. Or lose the bottle. Or give him too little or too much.

VASSA: What are we saying here?

MIKHAIL: That we can do something to protect the business from Prokhor.

VASSA: But he would need to have an attack first. And he carries that medicine with him. He took some this morning in front of me. He tried to hide it, but I saw.

MIKHAIL: He's started to take more and more lately. And he's added another one. I went to pay the pharmacy bill and the doctor told me to be sure that Prokhor understood that these medicines he was taking were very dangerous - together.

VASSA: What's the other medicine?

MIKHAIL: It's a little embarrassing to say—it's for his strength with the ladies.

VASSA: Oh god.

MIKHAIL: So if he took them both at the same time—or someone gave them to him together AND if the dosage was too high for both—

VASSA: — a mistake Lipa could make so easily.

MIKHAIL: Very easily. I'm surprised it hasn't happened before.

VASSA: We've come a long way, Mischa—you and I, a long way to this property and business and way of life. It would be a tragedy to lose it. A tragedy.

MIKHAIL: I totally agree Vassa Petrovna.

VASSA: Once again, Mikhail Vassilyev, you've shown how much I need you.

(MIKHAIL *goes to* VASSA *and bows in respect and kisses her hand. She strokes his head and kisses his brow. He exits. She looks at the perogi.*)

VASSA: Why is the cook making a big lunch? I hate wasting food!

(VASSA *picks up the perogi, on her way to yell at the cook, goes to the door and opens it,* PAVEL *falls into the room. He's been listening.*)

PAVEL: I was about to knock.

VASSA: What did you hear?

PAVEL: Something about a tragedy. You were talking about my life, weren't you, Mother? About Liudmila and me! And my affliction! Why must everyone fixate on my unhappiness? It's my own business.

(ANNA *enters, in a new, even more tasteful, outfit*)

ANNA: Mother, have you— (*Sees* PAVEL, *shuts up*)

PAVEL: What? Can't talk in front of me? Already? You just got here, Anna!!

VASSA: Oh, you make me tired! (*Exits*)

PAVEL: Don't stay here too long, dear sister. You'll get sucked in and won't be able to escape. And then you'll become One of Us again. It's already starting to happen. And it's very hard to deal with when you're an adult. I'm thirty-four and it's intolerable! Semyon is…Semyon, but he's unhappy, too.!

ANNA: But you and Semyon—at least you have each other.

PAVEL: Not any more. His wife controls him, totally, just as Mother always did. It's stifling here, Anna. I can't do anything. I have my affliction, of course. You are so beautiful! Look at these clothes! So stylish. But you… Oh my god, here comes Mephistopheles.

(PROKHOR *enters.*)

PAVEL: Make way for His Satanic Majesty!

PROKHOR: They're coming! If you want lunch, you better move fast.

(NATALYA *and* SEMYON *enter.*)

SEMYON: Anuita! So you met my Natalya.

NATALYA: Nice to see you again, Sister-in-law Anna.

SEMYON: My wife is formal. She's an Old-Believer. She was christened in an actual baptismal font. A very large one.

PROKHOR: Do they make them that big?

NATALYA: We're missing someone. Where is Liudmila? Pavel, where is your wife?

PAVEL: I don't know. (*About what he feels is the derision of the family*) They all want to be the death of me, Anna!

ANNA: Oh, Pasha. I'll protect you. (*She embraces him.*)

PROKHOR: (*To* SEMYON) She has become such a beauty! The making of a grand dame!

SEMYON: Isn't she wonderful?

NATALYA: (*About* ANNA) The colors she wears!

PROKHOR: It's called good taste.

NATALYA: Semyon, are you crying?

SEMYON: She looks like Mother. When we were little.

(MIKHAIL *enters.*)

MIKHAIL: Anna Zakharovna, let me greet you upon your return to your true hearth and home. Where is your Mother?

VASSA: (*Entering*) Here. Where did you all come from? This is supposed to be my office.

(LIUDMILA *rushes in, overplaying it a bit so that* VASSA *won't realize that they have already met and talked.*)

LIUDMILA: Anna! Anna!

ANNA: She knows.

VASSA: I know you already saw each other. Liuda, speak. No greeting for me?

LIUDMILA: Mother.

VASSA: Come here.

(LIUDMILA *comes to* VASSA *for a hug and* VASSA *grabs her and uses this moment to ask her about* PROKHOR.)

VASSA: I know everything. What are you doing?

LIUDMILA: (*Understanding what the question was about*) I don't know.

VASSA: Anna visited her father. Did anyone else? Semyon?

SEMYON: He's been sick, off and on, for so long, Mother.

PROKHOR: Oh, is he not well?
I wondered where he was.
I haven't seen him at dinner lately.

PAVEL: (*To* PROKHOR) You think you're so funny. But you're just mean.

PROKHOR: Was I talking to you—you bow without an arrow?

VASSA: That's enough!! I want this room cleared!! I don't want to see another person who's related to me for a full hour! Disperse!! Don't make me start counting—One, Two—NOT YOU, MISCHA, YOU STAY—Four, Five—

SEMYON: There's a big lunch being prepared. Let's go hurry it up in the kitchen.

PROKHOR: I'm not some child—

VASSA: *(In his face)* SIX—SEVEN—

NATALYA: *(To PROKHOR)* I'd go if I were you.

*(Everyone goes, leaving VASSA and MIKHAIL.)*

VASSA: You're smiling.

MIKHAIL: I got the third signature.

VASSA: Thank God. Who?

MIKHAIL: Father Yegor.

VASSA: How much did it cost us?

MIKHAIL: A thousand.

VASSA: *(Reeling from the amount)* Good God. He'll go straight to hell for that transaction. So something good has come out of this dreadful day after all.

MIKHAIL: So we're saved, then.

VASSA: Almost. Don't forget, Prokhor threatened to take his money out of the business.

*(Sound of offstage arguing—PAVEL and PROKHOR. LIUDMILA runs back in)*

LIUDMILA: Mama! Pavel and Prokhor are at it again! You'd better come!

*(They both get up wearily, to go and deal with the battle. As LIUDMILA exits back where she came from, she shouts to them)*

LIUDMILA: I'm afraid he'll give Uncle Prokhor a heart attack!

*(MIKHAIL and VASSA hear that at the same moment and look at each other with an icy satisfaction, and sit back down. The argument increases in volume. LIUDMILA re-enters, followed by PROKHOR.)*

LIUDMILA: Aren't you coming?

PROKHOR: Vassonka, I've endured quite enough, don't you think? Why can't you control your children?

VASSA: Because they've grown up.

PAVEL: *(Enters)* Oh, here you are. Telling on me to Mommy?

PROKHOR: Pavel Zakharovich—

PAVEL: Oh, don't you patronymic me. You want everyone here to think you're the injured party. And respectable. Hah!

PROKHOR: I've never hit a cripple.

PAVEL: Well, not since the last time you hit me, anyway.

LIUDMILA: They're starting up again! I can't stand it! I'm telling you I can't stand it!!

PAVEL: See what you've done? You've upset my *wife*. And she is *my wife*, in case you'd forgotten.

PROKHOR: You are going to bring me to physical violence. Vassa? Vassa Petrovna, I'm going to hit your son!

VASSA: Then do it. Liudmila, move over. *(She crosses to couch and sits down.)* There. *(Looks to* PAVEL *and* PROKHOR*)* All right, boys. Kill each other.

*(Long beat.* PAVEL *and* PROKHOR *don't know what to do)*

PROKHOR: This is absurd. *(He exits.)*

PAVEL: Now. Is that a man? I don't think so. Liudmila, aren't I better than that?

LIUDMILA: No! Leave me alone! I'm sick of both of you!

PAVEL: *(To* VASSA*)* Why, Mother? Why can't I love someone who loves me?

*(VASSA doesn't answer.* PAVEL *exits.)*

VASSA: Liuda, this can't go on.

LIUDMILA: Mother—

VASSA: I'm not your mother! I'm Pavel's mother!

LIUDMILA: Please, Mama, you're the only mother I've ever had. Don't reject me—I'll die, I swear I will. Look. look—If it weren't for Prokhor, maybe we could live in peace, Pavel and I. Not with love but with some kind of acceptance. It's Prokhor—Uncle Prokhor's presence enrages Pavel.

VASSA: And why is that?

LIUDMILA: Before I gave in, Pavel still wanted to kill him. They still fought all the time. I can't stand it, Mother. Mama—?

*(VASSA motions for LIUDMILA to come to her. VASSA kisses her on the forehead and gently sends her away)*

MIKHAIL: Liudmila—

VASSA: Let her go.
So, Mischa, we know what is at the center of our problems now.

MIKHAIL: What?

VASSA: Who.

MIKHAIL: Prokhor. Yes. He needs to be dealt with.

PROKHOR: *(Offstage)* Stop it! You foul little monkey! Stop following me!!

PAVEL: *(Offstage)* You're afraid of me!! Admit it!! You walked out on a fight!!

PROKHOR: *(Offstage)* I could crush you beneath my foot, if I wanted to!

PAVEL: *(Offstage)* Then do it!! Here. I'll lie down.

LIUDMILA: *(Offstage)* Pavel, what are you doing? Get off the floor!

PAVEL: *(Offstage)* You're taking his side! You want to protect him!

LIUDMILA: *(Offstage)* No, I want you to get off the floor. It's ridiculous!

PAVEL: *(Offstage)* Come on, Uncle Prokhor, my dear uncle—crush me beneath your foot!

PROKHOR: *(Offstage)* You cockroach!!

*(Sound of a struggle as* PAVEL *grabs* PROKHOR's *foot)*

PAVEL: LET GO OF MY FOOT!!

LIUDMILA: Prokhor! DON'T!!

*(Sound of the big man,* PROKHOR, *falling down)*

LIUDMILA: *(Offstage)* PAVEL, WHAT HAVE YOU DONE???

*(*MIKHAIL *and* VASSA *are listening, with hope—has this done* PROKHOR *in?)*

PROKHOR: *(Entering)* Really! This is beneath my dignity! I'm leaving!

*(*MIKHAIL *and* VASSA *realize* PROKHOR *is still alive.)*

PAVEL: *(Entering)* It's him!! She cares about that bag of sagging flesh!!

LIUDMILA: *(Entering)* I just want to live a normal life!! I don't care about anyone!

PROKHOR: *(Entering)* Vassa Petrovna! What are you going to do with your oldest son?!!

LIUDMILA: *(To* MIKHAIL*)* Father! What am I to do??

NATALYA: *(Entering)* Lunch is ready and where is everyone? The cook is furious!

SEMYON: *(Entering)* Natalya—let's stay out of all this. Everyone! Can't we get along?

PROKHOR: Semyon! Trying to be a peacemaker? You don't have the brains or the vocabulary!

ANNA: *(Entering)* What's going on down here? What's happened?

VASSA: Everything and nothing. Will I ever have any peace?

MIKHAIL: Vassa Petrovna needs to be left alone!

PAVEL: Oh, listen to the head dog. *(Barks at him)*

LIPA: *(Entering)* Excuse me. Hello? Excuse me.

VASSA: Lipa, go away!

MIKHAIL: Lipa, be quiet!

LIUDMILA: What are you doing here, Lipa?

NATALYA: Why aren't you with Father-in-law?

LIPA: Because—

SEMYON: See? I'm not the only one not working.

PAVEL: Do you ever work, Semyon?

LIPA: I just—

SEMYON: How would you know what work is?

LIPA: I need to tell you—

VASSA: Oh, everyone just go!!

NATALYA: But lunch—

VASSA: —will be silent!!

LIPA: Vassa Petrov—

VASSA: Silence!!

*(She exits and everyone else does, too. In spite of* LIPA'S *effort to get their attention)*

LIPA: Semyon?

*(*SEMYON *re-enters.)*

SEMYON: What?

*(*LIPA *whispers something in* SEMYON'S *ear.* SEMYON *is amazed and calls to his brother)*

SEMYON: Pavel! Pavel!

(PAVEL *re-enters.*)

SEMYON: Father's dead.

PAVEL: Father's dead?

SEMYON: He's dead.

*(Beat)*

PAVEL: I'm free!!

SEMYON: We're free!!

(SEMYON *swings a bewildered* LIPA *around.* PAVEL, *always competitive, swings* LIPA *around. Lights down on this celebration)*

### END OF ACT ONE

# ACT TWO

## Scene One

*(NATALYA. SEMYON enters with trousers on and wearing his robe, the robe covering what will be revealed as pants too tight to close. He looks around to be sure they are alone and then crosses to her.)*

SEMYON: Natalya! *(Opening his robe)* Look! This is my good suit!

NATALYA: Here. Come here. *(He crosses to her.)* They must have shrunk.

SEMYON: What am I going to do? Father's funeral is tomorrow!

NATALYA: Come over here. Sit down.

*(They sit on the couch. He leans back and she tries to button his fly—it definitely looks as though she is giving him a blow job. Prokhor passes, looks, retreats.)*

NATALYA: I've almost got it. Suck in some more.

*(This gets the buttons closed, but SEMYON can't breathe.)*

NATALYA: Stand up. Can you breathe?

SEMYON: *(Constricted)* Almost.

NATALYA: You look so handsome, Senya! You'll just have to hold your breath until tomorrow. And some day, very, very soon, you'll be going to a tailor and getting lots of new suits—that won't shrink!

SEMYON: My beautiful Natasha, my Nanooshka. What would I do without you

(ANNA *enters, smoking a cigarette.*)

ANNA: Mother's not here? Good.

(*She smokes enthusiastically as she goes through papers on the desk.* NATALYA *coughs in response to the cigarette smoke. She coughs again.*)

NATALYA: Sister-in-law Anna, the smell of cigarettes make me ill. And it's disrespectful to the dead.

SEMYON: Natalya, let's go. I need to take these pants off.

PROKHOR: Don't you two have a bedroom?

NATALYA: How dare you?

SEMYON: Natalya, let's go. Please.

(SEMYON *gets* NATALYA *to exit with him.*)

ANNA: Where did Semyon find her?

PROKHOR: Oh, she found *him*. Pavel had this idea of buying old icons from the Old Believers across the river. Icons do well on the antiques market. He got Semyon to do the buying and that's how our poor, dull Semyon met the only woman dimmer than he is. And, immediately, they recognized each other as being from the same tribe—The Stupidians. So, of course, they got married. So they could propogate the world with Stupidian babies.

ANNA: Does her family have any money?

PROKHOR: Why? Do you think that Semyon will give you some of his inheritance since his wife is rich?

ANNA: Is she rich?

PROKHOR: Well, they're *Old Believers*. They believe in a Pure Christian Life. So, Of course they're loaded. But I don't think she's going to get any of it. Evidently, in

that Pure Christian Way, they have been *fruitful* and
*multiplied*. Her mother is still getting pregnant. The old
man is as insatiable as Tolstoy. Or me.

ANNA: Semyon wants to move to town.

PROKHOR: So Senya and that heifer have plans. That
explains what I heard coming from their bedroom last
night: "I can't explain it quite, but, anyway, Senia—"
I'm being Natalya. This is Natalya. "I am lying in my
lilac velvet dressing gown, and underneath is nothing
but a black lace negligee and I am sitting on a perfect
quelque-chose—"

ANNA: What? Wait. Was she trying to say "chaise-
longue?"

PROKHOR: "May wee." But there's more: "And different
people, Senia, they are coming to visit. There are the
police chief, the judges, the mayor, the entire town!
And everybody envies you, as they look at me, *moi*,
and they say, 'Well done, Zheleznov!' and "Look what
a wonderful wife he has—oh yes!'
Oh, I see I've made you sick. Well, I have the bedroom
next to theirs. Imagine what I hear when they're
making love.

ANNA: Oh stop! The image of both of them so—. I
mean, I was shocked at how chubby Semyon has
gotten.

PROKHOR: "Chubby"? He's positively bovine. He
matches her in shape, you may have noticed. What's
amazing is that he's achieved that without her layers
of skirts and whatever else she's got under there. They
get up in the morning, both of them, and spend the day
grazing. The cook sees them coming, but you can't hide
everything. I am sick to death of all of them. I am going
to take my money and leave—leave this den of thieves
we call a family.

ANNA: What would you do with your money?

PROKHOR: Looking for some help from me? I'd go to Moscow. I have the product of a love affair—a son.

ANNA: What?

PROKHOR: You don't think I could've fathered a son? My dear lady, I'm sure there are many out there—a legion. And I could still father a son. My heart has some weakness, but everything else works. And very well.

ANNA: Are you going to legally—

PROKHOR: —acknowledge him? What? You want more family? Aren't we enough?

*(SEMYON enters and PROKHOR lets ANNA go.)*

SEMYON: Anna, my Natalya is very upset.

ANNA: I'm sorry Semyon. We're both sorry.

PROKHOR: I thought you were supposed to go to the factory.

SEMYON: Father's dead. I'm in mourning. I'll work here.

PROKHOR: Semyon, what about a game of cards? Come on. I'll behave, I promise.

SEMYON: Why not. I've worked enough today.

PROKHOR: We need a fourth. I'll go get Liudmila. *(PROKHOR exits)*

SEMYON: *(Calling after PROKHOR)* Is that a good idea? *(To ANNA)* Uncle Prokhor should just leave Liudmila alone.

ANNA: How long has he been…playing around with her?

SEMYON: *(With pleasure)* "Playing around?" I was waiting to hear what you'd call it. I knew you'd know

the sophisticated term for it. Well, he's been trying
to *play around* with Liudmila for a few years, but
last night was the only time that the *playing* around
actually came to something.

ANNA: And what does Pavel do about it? Does he ever
talk to you about just leaving?

SEMYON: Pavel? He'd never leave this place. I don't
think he'd survive outside that door. And what does
he do about his wife and his uncle? You've heard
it! He just yells. And Uncle Prokhor yells back and
occasionally hits him. To Hell with Uncle Prokhor! He
gets away with so much. He always has—he's been
spoiled—a big grown up baby. Father and Mother
always did all the work. Uncle Prokhor has done
whatever he wanted to all his life.

ANNA: He has a son. Whom he is going to legally
recognize.

SEMYON: A son? Well, good. Let him bring the boy here
and he can run the business. I don't want to. We sell
dirt! We sell peat for stoves that are going out of date.
And then we dig clay and make tiles and bricks from
that dirt, and sell those. I say let Mother and Mikhailo
scrounge for the kopecks there. All right—I have to tell
you something—a secret. I'm going to open a jewelry
store in town, right on the main street. And there will
be a sign: "Semyon Zheleznov's Jewelry Shop!"

*(Offstage, a few rooms away, the sound of two males voices
bursting with rage—PROKHOR and PAVEL. The words are
indistinguishable but the anger can be heard.)*

PAVEL & PROKHOR: It's a soft sound— "Jewelry!" So
soft. "Je". My apartment will be right above the store,
with Natalya. I'll buy a harmonium and learn to play
it. "Je!" That's my destiny.

LIUDMILA: *(Running in)* Anna, come quickly. See if you can stop them!

ANNA: Who?

LIUDMILA: Uncle Prokhor is threatening to fight Pavel. With fists.

SEMYON: Here we are, thank you very much. And I was talking about "je".

LIUDMILA: Anna, go on!

ANNA: Go where? They could hit me! You'd better go!

SEMYON: *(Exiting)* Why do I have to be the policeman? *(Offstage)* Anna says stop it!

LIUDMILA: I wish Uncle Prokhor would just kill Pavel and get it over with. I feel so sorry for him. He is so repulsive!

ANNA: Which one? Listen to me—I've been in this house two days and I'm already getting so mean. What's the fight about this time?

LIUDMILA: Pavel said he wouldn't let me go to play cards, so I started laughing. The next thing I knew, he pushed me and started shouting, then Uncle Prokhor grabbed him by the hair.

ANNA: It's a nightmare!

VASSA: *(Entering)* What is that noise about? This house is in mourning! Your father is lying upstairs—dead!

LIUDMILA: Oh, Mama, see if you can do something with them.

VASSA: What have you done now?

LIUDMILA: Nothing! It's just Pavel and Uncle Prokhor, arguing again.

VASSA: Why can't you be nice to Pavel, just for a moment—

LIUDMILA: I can't! You know better than anyone, I can't
be nice! You told me yourself—it's hard to trick a man.

VASSA: Not in that way. They always want to believe
that you love them. Just calm them down… They're
both idiots. Go, just go!

LIUDMILA: *(Exiting)* Why do I have to go? *(Offstage)*
Stop it! Stop it! You both make me sick!

ANNA: Does this happen often?

VASSA: Nearly every day for three years in a row. And
I feel this pressure on my chest as if they've all got their
hands around my heart and are squeezing it as hard as
they can. Times like this, I think I could just do them all
in. Every single one of them. And then…I am so sorry
for Pavel! I can't help it.

ANNA: Liudmila's life isn't very good, either, Mama.

VASSA: Her? She'll be fine.

ANNA: How do you know?

VASSA: I raised her to be like me. You, too, Anna.
But the boys—they refuse to be like me. I'm just a
"mother."

ANNA: I've found out a couple of things that are very
alarming.

VASSA: What?

ANNA: Semyon is moving to town, buying a
harmonium and a jewelry store.

VASSA: Oh god.

ANNA: Pavel, too. Semyon says he'll never do it. But
Pavel told me himself—he's leaving—doesn't know
where, but he's leaving.

VASSA: And what would they be planning for me? A
little shack in Finland? How do they think *I'll* live?
And the future of their children, if they have any.

They'll be destitute. We might as well be serfs again.
None of you know what that life is like. I was born
into slavery, in the dirt. What my mother suffered, my
father. Why did you never have grandparents? They
were worked to death. What good is Emancipation
when you have nothing? Poverty is the slavery! And
you all will be living in it soon!

(NATALYA, PROKHOR, SEMYON *enter excitedly.*)

SEMYON: Natalya, stop it!

PROKHOR: Would you shut this stupid idiot up!

NATALYA: Except for me, who else is speaking the
truth?

SEMYON: Natalya, calm down. What has all this to do
with you, with us? You have to remember— "je!"

VASSA: What is it now?

PROKHOR: Your least favorite daughter-in-law is
meddling— "sill voo pley!"

NATALYA: (*To* PROKHOR) All this is your fault. You've
made Pasha become violent!

PROKHOR: Do you know that poor, misled, peace-
loving Pasha, just threatened me with a knife? A
knife! A person like that shouldn't be allowed near
any cutlery at all! Not even a fork! From now on, only
spoons. Only spoons!

(LIUDMILA *enters, silently.*)

NATALYA: It is your fault.

VASSA: Semyon, can't you control this wife of yours? If
you don't, I will!

SEMYON: Natalya, don't upset Mother.

NATALYA: Senia, I have to say it! I must speak it out
loud! The reason you made Pasha violent, Uncle
Prokhor—the reason is you ruined Liudmila.

PROKHOR: "Ruined?" You are such an idiot! Don't you know, she did it before she was married. *(Notices* LIUDMILA*)* Oh.

LIUDMILA: Well, tell us, Uncle Prokhor, what exactly was it that I did before I was married?

VASSA: *(Strictly, quietly)* Liuda. Stop. Shut up.

PROKHOR: *Bella figlia del amore.*

LIUDMILA: Tell me. Tell everyone. What is this "it" that I did before I was married?

PROKHOR: *(Exiting)* They made me say it!

LIUDMILA: *(To the exiting* PROKHOR*)* Now we see who you really are, Uncle Prokhor—a coward right down to the bone!

VASSA: I told you! Be quiet.

LIUDMILA: It doesn't matter, Mama! Pavel will find out now—he will find out everything!

SEMYON: *(To his wife)* Let's go! They're getting into territory—

LIUDMILA: There goes Natalya. She blabs everything and then sneaks away.

SEMYON: *(To* NATALYA*)* You just remember— "je!" That's all you need.

*(*SEMYON *and* NATALYA *exit.)*

LIUDMILA: Oh, if I could leave my skin entirely just to escape all of this—to escape!

PAVEL: *(Entering, his forehead in a bandage)* Mother, give me some money.

LIUDMILA: Oh, you are attractive! Oh, my god…

PAVEL: *(Quietly)* Are you a mother to me? Anna, tell her…let me go.

ANNA: *(To* VASSA*)* My advice, exactly Mama—let him go!

VASSA: Liudmila, go away! Pavel, you, too. Go! Now!

(LIUDMILA *and* PAVEL *exit.* LIPA *enters.)*

LIPA: Anna Zakharovna, your Uncle Prokhor asks you to come.

VASSA: What are you doing here? Mikhail is looking for you!

ANNA: Do you know what for?

LIPA: He is not feeling well. It's his heart.

ANNA: His heart?

VASSA: He's had this before.

LIPA: Short breath.

VASSA: Shortness of breath. Olimpiada knows, you see. Go Anna, go take care of Uncle Prokhor.

ANNA: I'll go. I don't know what I can do.

(ANNA *exits.* VASSA *signals for* LIPA *to stay.* MIKHAIL *appears—he and* VASSA *exchange a look.)*

VASSA: You talk to her.

(VASSA *exits, leaving* MIKHAIL *alone with* LIPA.*)*

MIKHAIL: Well?

LIPA: I won't do it.

MIKHAIL: You have to.

LIPA: I can't. I'm scared.

MIKHAIL: Scared of what?

LIPA: God.

MIKHAIL: Is God scarier than living on the streets?

LIPA: His judgment. I've done other sins. It's a human being we're talking about after all.

MIKHAIL: Well. To strangle your son is not a sin, but to kill someone else is? Isn't a child a human being?

LIPA: A child! I did it out of pity!

MIKHAIL: And fear. Your fear. You were protecting yourself, Lipa. That's how the world would see it. And that's how God sees it, too. And Prokhor. Prokhor— he knows all about what you did. But unlike God, he might talk about it to someone.

LIPA: But you know it, too! And Vassa Petrovna. What do I need to do—poison everyone? I should just poison myself and end all this misery!

MIKHAIL: Suicide is the worst sin. Even the scriptures don't write about it, it's so bad. A great sin against God.

LIPA: All I want is to be left alone. I can't do it. I have to go—

MIKHAIL: Go where? Out the front door to live on the road? Do not tempt desperate people, Olimpiada. People whose lives and welfare are at stake. People who have control of your fate. I wasn't born to be a murderer, but I will not sink into poverty. Just pour together as much as you can from the two medicines and give it to him! And it is not a poison, it's a medicine! Now go! Lipa, you are young and you need to live. I know you value your freedom. You can go wherever you want to—I'll help. Lipa, you cannot get through life without sinning. A lot of us tried and couldn't do it! Think of your Saviour's pleasure at forgiving you. That's what he's there for. Lipa, if you don't sin, you don't need to confess. If you don't confess, there is no salvation. Now, go DO IT! Are you going to DO IT?

LIPA: Yes. (*Exits*)

MIKHAIL: Look at her—living in her religious melodrama, her own little passion play. Such trash!

(PAVEL *enters.*)

PAVEL: Where is Mother?

MIKHAIL: Went to Zakhar Ivanovich.

PAVEL: Whom were you talking with?

MIKHAIL: With myself.

PAVEL: What a good companion you found, then. But I'd watch him, if I were you. He's not to be trusted.

MIKHAIL: Thanks for the warning! I accept it as a reward for my life of service to you.

PAVEL: Consider it charity. You're on the street with a cup and I throw in a couple of kopecks. Catch!

(PAVEL *throws a couple of kopecks at* MIKHAIL *and exits.* VASSA *re-enters to talk to* MIKHAIL. *After a beat,* SEMYON *and* NATALYA *enter, looking for food*)

VASSA: What are these kopecks doing on the floor? Pick them up, Mikhail. Take care of the kopecks and the rubles will take care of themselves. Zakhar used to say that, God rest his soul. *(To* SEMYON *and* NATALYA*)* There are eleven rooms in this house! Why does everyone have to be here?

SEMYON: We heard there were little sandwiches.

*(Sees his mother's look and exits)*

SEMYON: I'll go. Natalya— "je!" *(He exits.)*

VASSA: *(About* SEMYON's *"je")* What is that? What did he say?

NATALYA: *(Covering for her husband)* Something…I don't know. *(She exits.)*

VASSA: I hope they *don't* have children. *(To* MIKHAIL*)* Did you finish your little talk with Lipa?

MIKHAIL: Yes.

VASSA: Is she upstairs with Prokhor?

MIKHAIL: Yes.

VASSA: So we wait.

(ANNA *enters.*)

ANNA: I think we should send for the doctor. Prokhor is very bad. Lipa gave him his medicine but then he got worse instead of better.

VASSA: Where is Lipa now?

ANNA: She's huddled on the stairs.

VASSA: Go get her, Mischa.

MIKHAIL: Lipa, get in here!

ANNA: I can't get her to move. It's not her fault. Shouldn't we send for a doctor?

(LIPA *enters.*)

VASSA: (*To* LIPA) What have you done?

LIPA: (*Pointing to* MIKHAIL) I did? It's him. It's all him.

VASSA: Listen to me! It's not the first time you've given him his medicine, is it? Don't you know how much he needs?

LIPA: Let me go, *please!*

ANNA: (*In fear*) Why won't you call for the doctor? Prokhor's going to die!

(VASSA *turns to* ANNA *and stares at her.*)

VASSA: That's possible. He's old and he's sick. (*Back to* LIPA) Do you know that for a mistake like this, you can go to jail? How could you make such a mistake?

LIPA: (*Doesn't understand anything*) What's going to happen? What's going to happen to me?

MIKHAIL: You, stupid girl! Give me a minute with her—

VASSA: *(To* LIPA*)* Shut up! Sit here! *(Then, to* ANNA*)* The girl gave him the wrong medicine. It happens! The master of the house is dead, there is chaos everywhere, the girl was looking after everything, running her legs off—

ANNA: You mean if the police come.

MIKHAIL: *(Alarmed that* ANNA *knows more than he thought she did)* What is she saying? Vassa Petrovna—

VASSA: Be quiet. Everyone be quiet.

NATALYA: *(Running in)* Come quickly. Uncle Prokhor—

ANNA: *(Fearing the worst)* —died?

NATALYA: No! How can you even say that? But he did give me quite a scare. He's sitting up in his bed, groaning and hiccupping.

VASSA: Hiccupping? He's hiccupping?

NATALYA: Yes. But I think he will be fine. Come on, Anna. We don't want to leave him alone.

VASSA: Yes, go, Anna. Help your Uncle Prokhor. With his hiccups.

*(*ANNA *follows* NATALYA. *They both exit.* VASSA *turns on* LIPA*)*

VASSA: He's alive! He's alive!

MIKHAIL: *(To* LIPA*)* This mistake will cost you!

VASSA: *(To* LIPA*)* Get out of my sight!

LIPA: *(About* MIKHAIL*)* I did it the way he told me!

VASSA: Go to your room!

LIPA: I'll never have any peace on this earth. What have I done? My life can't bear another sin. Oh, God. Oh, God. Oh. *(Exits)*

VASSA: *(Turns on* MIKHAIL*)* Why didn't it work?

MIKHAIL: What does Anna know? She's talking like she knows.

VASSA: Don't worry about Anna. But your doctor friend is a total idiot. He's got us involved in a murder and the victim's not even dead!

MIKHAIL: Maybe those medicines take more time

VASSA: He's hiccupping! Hiccups aren't fatal. Run after Lipa. She must not be allowed to speak—preferably about anything. You will have to watch her every minute of the day. And night. Don't let her have a moment's peace!

*(*ANNA *enters.)*

ANNA: He's calm now. I guess we don't need a doctor.

VASSA: Why are you looking at me like that?

ANNA: I'm beginning to understand something.

*(*PAVEL *enters.)*

PAVEL: Mama! He tried to rip off one of my ears! I think he did some damage!

VASSA: I'm sick to death of all of you! *(Exits)*

PAVEL: Anna…

*(*PAVEL *goes to* ANNA *for comfort. She accepts him.)*

PAVEL: I told you not to stay or you'd get sucked in. Well… You're up to your waist now. Soon it will be over your head.

*(Sound of a scream, then* LIUDMILA *enters)*

ANNA: Who's screaming?

LIUDMILA: It's awful. It's so awful. I've been so mean.

PAVEL: But I forgive you, Liuda. I love you.

LIUDMILA: Get away from me!

PAVEL: But you just said-

LIUDMILA: I'm not talking about you! It's Lipa—I was so mean to her. And now she's dead.

ANNA: What?

PAVEL: Look at you! You're crying for a dead girl. And you won't even look at me!

(PAVEL *exits, almost running into* VASSA *who is entering.*)

VASSA: Lipa's hanged herself. Natalya found her. Mischa's cutting her down.

ANNA: Oh my god.

LIUDMILA: I've been so mean to her.

VASSA: Liuda! Be quiet! We all need to be quiet. If even for a moment.

(MIKHAIL *enters.*)

LIUDMILA: Oh, Daddy!

(*She runs to him for comfort—he holds her at bay*)

MIKHAIL: Don't—don't touch me right now. (*To* VASSA) I've put her on her bed.

LIUDMILA: Who's going to dress her body? I can't. I just can't.

VASSA: (*To* MIKHAIL) We have to report the death. Well, go, go!

(MIKHAIL *exits.* VASSA *speaks to* LIUDMILA.)

VASSA: Stop blubbering! And don't feel guilty. It's useless. It's not going to help her. Besides, we were all mean to her. But we also gave her a home she would have never had. She had no people—no one. We saved her for a few years, like a stray dog who's doomed.

ANNA: A "stray dog"?

VASSA: You don't believe me? Stroll through the village sometime and look at the young orphaned girls and their lives. Slavery—might as well be. And beatings. And starvation. And worse. Now, all of you leave me alone. I'm going to wait for Mikhail Vasilievich to get back. We'll have to deal with the arrangements.

(LIUDMILA *exits, but* ANNA *hesitates.*)

ANNA: Mother—

VASSA: We do things for our children, hard things sometimes. How far should a mother go? How far would you go?

ANNA: I would do what's necessary.

VASSA: Hand me that shawl and go.

(ANNA *takes her shawl and puts it around* VASSA. ANNA *exits as* VASSA *pulls it around her and waits in the dark* PAVEL *enters quietly.*)

PAVEL: Where's Liudmila?

VASSA: I don't know.

(PAVEL *crosses to his mother and embraces her or kneels next to her and she embraces him—some old posture they had when he was a child*)

VASSA: What are you doing?

PAVEL: I'm looking for comfort.

VASSA: Your ear will be fine. Come here. Let me look at it. *(She puts her arms around him and rocks him).* What am I going to do with you?

PAVEL: *(Breaks the embrace, stands and looks at her)* What am I going to do with you, Mama? Now that Father's dead? *(Caresses her cheek)* My little mamachka.

*(End of Scene One)*

## Scene Two

*(The next day, day of Zahkar's funeral. And* LIPA's.
SEMYON *is dressed in mourning-in his pants that are too
tight. He checks to see if he's alone and then undoes his pants
and breathes with relief. He feels the samovar. It's cold. He
roots around for something to eat. He finds a stash of cookies
that Natalya left and just as he's about to put one in his
mouth, his mother enters)*

VASSA: What are you doing?

*(*VASSA *slaps the cookie out of* SEMYON's *hand)*

VASSA: You just took Holy Communion!

SEMYON: I've been to two funerals. It makes me
hungry. Besides, it's just a little cookie.

VASSA: You tell your wife that you desecrated the body
and blood of Jesus by eating some broken cookie.

*(No answer from* SEMYON*)*

VASSA: That shut you up, I see. Clean up here. Where is
Natalya? She disappeared after the service.

SEMYON: She doesn't feel well.
Is there anything to eat? I mean, when the hour is
passed?

VASSA: Your father is dead and all you can think about
is your stomach?

*(*ANNA *enters, also dressed in mourning)*

SEMYON: Anna, did you see any old friends at the
funerals? I think I did.

ANNA: We never had friends, Semyon!

SEMYON: Don't snap at me, Anna.

ANNA: I couldn't sleep last night. I thought I heard
someone walking around.

SEMYON: They say that suicides are doomed to walk at night in the place they killed themselves.

VASSA: I don't know. Maybe.

ANNA: Don't say that, Mother.

SEMYON: Oh, she doesn't believe it. Stop pretending you believe in any of this, Mother. Your only religion is money.

VASSA: (Inoffensively) Semyonushka, you are such a moron, sometimes! Why do you think your father and I gathered all this money? Huh? For our children, we thought. But not one of them deserves any of it. You couldn't even give me a grandson, you, Mister I-Want-To-Eat-My-Wife-Is-Sick-Boo-Hoo!

SEMYON: I had a child!

VASSA: He wasn't healthy and you had him by a servant girl who was more of a moron than you are.

SEMYON: A servant girl you threw at me! You threw Olimpiada at me, Mother. "Lipa, see what Semyon needs," "Lipa, go for a ride with Semyon." "Take Semyon's tea up to his room."

VASSA: I wanted to protect you!

SEMYON: From what?

VASSA: From the diseases that killed your father! From lecherous behavior!

SEMYON: Lipa gave birth to my son. So I did give you a grandchild.

VASSA: But the child was born dead.

SEMYON: (Stands up) He wasn't born dead, Mother. I've been waiting to say this to you. She did it herself. She told my Natalya everything—a long time ago. And don't lie about it anymore, Mother! You frightened Lipa so much somehow so that she strangled her own baby. My son. And then for the rest of her short life, you held it over her. And that was why she strangled herself. That's the truth!

ANNA: How can you say these…obscenities, Semyon? It's terrible, what you're saying….

SEMYON: It is a mistake, Anna Zahkarovna, taking Mother's side. It won't get you anything! *(He exits.)*

VASSA: These accusations could kill a weaker woman. Luckily, I'm not sensitive.

ANNA: Is Semyon telling the truth?

VASSA: She was never right. In the head. She was always unstable.

ANNA: Was the baby his?

VASSA: What baby? Do you see a grave for a baby, anywhere? That's in the past, all in the past. Poor Lipa. May she rest in peace. But we, the living, have to go on and take care of our own, yes? I've tried to save my children. I've tried to save them from themselves— that's the most thankless job of all. And, you see, they hate me. Anna, you will be in this same state someday—with your own children.

ANNA: I hope not.

VASSA: What makes you think you'll be spared? So now look at this fool—your dear brother Semyon! I tried to save his health by letting him have a mistress at home. And now it's a big sin and he shoves it in my face. But he, the idiot caught something bad in the village, and has, no doubt, given it to his wife. And she's probably barren because of it.

ANNA: But, Mother, I need to know—is it true that Lipa had Semyon's child and—

VASSA: Even if it is, so what? What should I have done?

ANNA: I don't know. But it's so hard to justify—

VASSA: Every child that is born into a family can make a legal claim on the property even products of someone's philanderings. So everyone's share gets a little smaller. And soon you watch your children become the owners of nothing! What do you think life is? About tea and morality? Morality is for the rich, Anna. I'll tell you what life is—food, shelter, heat and enough money to pay for them, again and again. So you won't starve, you won't be out in the elements, and you won't freeze—all of which you could easily do, in a week, outside that door. *(Long beat)* We have to protect what we have or others will take it. What do you want? To be moral and upstanding? Or to survive?

*(Beat)*

ANNA: Prokhor has a son whom he's going to legally recognize. He's written him two letters. One to invite him here to see this house and the other to sign some papers.

VASSA: When??? When did he mail them? How do you know about it? Anna, Anuita, do NOT play with me!

*(ANNA takes out two letters.)*

VASSA: You have them!

ANNA: Both letters.

VASSA: So they haven't been mailed!!

*(Beat)*

ANNA: I think they shouldn't be mailed.

VASSA: They cannot be mailed! Ever! You are so smart. You see, you're a woman! It's not the dogs that guard the house. It's us. Now, how much do you want for them?

ANNA: Nothing.

VASSA: What do you want for them both? Name a figure.

ANNA: If I give them to you, I'm protecting my home.
And my children's home. Isn't that right? Isn't that
right, Mother? Or are you still "considering it?"

VASSA: Yes, yes. You're protecting your home. Here.
With me. I swear it.

ANNA: On what?

VASSA: On my heart. Which you don't think I have. On
my mother's heart. On her mother's. And on and on.

ANNA: Here are the letters.

VASSA: That was good bargaining. But you fell for the
soppy speech at the end. You've got to watch that.
You've got to toughen up. No hurt, no shame. I'll tell
you what hurts. Stupidity! And shame—you can't be
ashamed of anything. Protect your children and protect
them from themselves. Just remember that! "Oh, I want
my children to make their own decisions." Well, look
around you. Pavel decided to marry Liudmila. Semyon
decided to seduce and impregnate Lipa and then
marry Natalya. You married a drunk. And so did I. If it
takes sin to save your children, then sin, by all means.

ANNA: When I came here, I thought I was better than
you.

VASSA: It's all right to think like that! That's the way…
it's handed down. If you make a mistake, I'll let you
know.

ANNA: Well, what about this? Uncle Prokhor will get
well, write more letters, and mail them, by himself. Or
he'll ask me to send them by registered mail and, then,
where would I get the receipts?

VASSA: Oh, we have plenty of them in my office. And
we've done it before. It's nothing. When your father
had a mistress in town, we used to do the same—
intercept, rewrite, redirect. We just need to make sure

Prokhor doesn't find someone else to mail them for him.

ANNA: Of course. I'll make sure of that.

VASSA: Watch out for Liudmila! She can be persuaded. She has a soft heart. She still believes people can be good.

ANNA: Poor girl.

VASSA: Just remember that Prokhor's money will be for your children.

*(The door opens and* NATALYA *comes in. She is weak and pale.)*

NATALYA: Tea is ready.

VASSA: Why are you in here? You look like a big, tired egg. A week after Easter.

NATALYA: Nobody laid the table.

VASSA: Do it yourself. Where is Pavel?

NATALYA: I was looking for him. I think he's in his room. I mean, his and Liudmila's room.

VASSA: You're such a joke.

NATALYA: Vassa Petrovna! I am your son's wife! "Je." "Je."

VASSA: What are you saying? "Je." What is that word?

NATALYA: Something that Semyon and I share.

VASSA: I'm glad you remember who you're married to, now and then.

NATALYA: I hear you talking and talking, Mother-in-Law. But you will not upset me. Anymore.

VASSA: Anna, will you find Pavel for me?

*(*ANNA *exits.* VASSA *turns on* NATALYA*.)*

VASSA: What do you mean by "anymore?"

NATALYA: Well, things have changed since Father-in-Law, may he rest in peace, passed away.

VASSA: What do you think has changed, Natalya?

NATALYA: Well, I know something about the law. And so does Semyon.

VASSA: I'd be quiet, if I were you, you black snowball with a rock in it! Finish your work!

(VASSA *exits and* PAVEL *enters.*)

NATALYA: You smell like wine.

PAVEL: Hmmp? I wonder— (*Breathes on her*) — whyyyyyy.

NATALYA: This is an important day. So I think you should know everything.

PAVEL: Ooo! Important!? What can it be? A Saint's name day? No, that's every day. There's so many of them. And they all live in this house. Saint Semyon. Saint Prokhor. Saint Liudmila…

NATALYA: I have to tell you something because I am your friend, Pavel. I want you to always remember that.

PAVEL: All right.

NATALYA: Your Liudmila—

PAVEL: Saint Liudmila.

NATALYA: —slept with your Uncle Prokhor.

(*Beat*)

PAVEL: I know.

NATALYA: Oh, Pasha, I am so sorry for you.

PAVEL: You feel sorry for everybody. So what's the point?

NATALYA: We are so alike, you and I.

PAVEL: Oh! Are you a freak? I didn't know that!

NATALYA: I mean, our characters are similar. We are both smart—

PAVEL: Oh! Are you smart? I really didn't know that.

NATALYA: Don't make jokes now! You mother thinks I'm stupid. I am not allowed to be a mistress of the house. I am your brother's wife and look, I live as if I were a servant. My word means nothing.

PAVEL: I don't give a damn about any of that!

NATALYA: Why not? You, yourself have no freedom. Just like all of us!

PAVEL: It's finished now! Today's an important day—just as you said. I will let them know who I am. They're not dealing with some naive country girl who can be pushed around. I'll go to town…to Moscow… everywhere! To hell with you! With your house, your land, your everything! I want nothing! Nothing at all. I am sick and tired of it all!

(LIUDMILA *enters*.)

PAVEL: Except you.

LIUDMILA: Anna is bringing Uncle Prokhor down for tea. Get a chair for him.

PAVEL: Who? Me? Let him sit on the floor.

NATALYA: My Semyon told me that Uncle Prokhor was very tired and shouldn't be disturbed.

(ANNA *enters with* PROKHOR, *helping him*.)

PROKHOR: I said I was exhausted but this lovely creature insisted I come down for some tea. With our loving family.

ANNA: Can someone help me? Semyon, I can see you— stop eavesdropping and help me here.

SEMYON: *(Entering from his hiding place)* Yes, commander! We have another commander! Who made you boss?

PROKHOR: Oh, Semyon. Wake up. Can't you recognize a power shift when you see it?

PAVEL: *(To* PROKHOR*)* Should I tell him that I am going to put two cats into his pigeon loft tonight?

LIUDMILA: Pavel! Stop teasing Uncle Prokhor! It always ends the same way!

PAVEL: She spoke to me! *(To* PROKHOR*)* And not to you, you old piece of dung.

LIUDMILA: Uncle Prokhor—

PAVEL: "Uncle"! Isn't that nice? She still calls him "Uncle." Because we're a family.

PROKHOR: You insolent little twit—I could squash you like a bug.

ANNA: He's just trying to get you upset. Because he knows your heart is bad.

PROKHOR: Don't tell him that, Anna! He'll do it on purpose! Because he wants me dead! Everyone wants me dead, except you, Anna - you and Liuda. Isn't that right Liudmila?

LIUDMILA: No one wants you dead.

ANNA: That's right.

PAVEL: Oh, come on, Sister Anna—You care if he lives or dies? This old, worn-out piece of flaccid skin?

PROKHOR: You will not upset me. You're a *nonentity*. And in a week or so, there will be some surprises for you all.

SEMYON: Are you marrying Uncle Prokhor now? He's Liudmila's.

PAVEL: Semyon! Shut up!! Shut up!!!!!

ANNA: Pavel!! Calm down!! Do you want to give Uncle Prokhor a heart attack!

PAVEL: She said it again! Are you trying to give me ideas? That's proof positive you're over your head, dear sister. The bog has engulfed you. You'll never be able to see or breathe freely again.

PROKHOR: Let him talk! Do you think, for one moment, I'll let him do anything?

SEMYON: Anna, what are you doing? I can't figure out what you're doing.

ANNA: What are you talking about?

NATALYA: You, Sister Anna, are cut out. Of the Will. So you're trying to get Uncle Prokhor on your side. That's what she's doing , Semyon.

SEMYON: I don't think so.

PAVEL: What does it matter? It won't last long. Nothing will last long!

SEMYON: *(Taking the booze away from* PAVEL*)* You have had enough to drink, Pavel.

PROKHOR: *(To* LIUDMILA*)* What is going to happen here in a week or so—amazing!

LIUDMILA: Nothing will happen. Nothing ever changes.

PAVEL: *(To* PROKHOR*)* Something will happen. Today. I will ask you…to go directly to Hell! And you'll have to go. Because you'll have no other home! And Hell, Uncle, Hell is the only place that will take you in.

*(*MIKHAIL *and* VASSA *enter.)*

ANNA: Pavel! That is so disrespectful!

PROKHOR: You, little cockroach!

PAVEL: "Disrespectful?" Oh, what a precious word! "Remove the knife from my throat—it's disrespectful!"

PROKHOR: Don't tell him anything more! He'll push me over the edge on purpose!

ANNA: *(To* PAVEL*)* Pavel, this is serious! The doctor said he'll die if he has another attack.

LIUDMILA: Anna, what do you keep telling him for?

SEMYON: I see what you're up to.

PAVEL: I'm watching you, sister Anna.
Glug, glug, glug. She's slipped beneath the surface. We shall see her no more. Bye-bye.

PROKHOR: Don't worry. I'm calm now. I won't let him upset me.

NATALYA: You all are acting like Pasha's some kind of dangerous villain! How could you?

PROKHOR: *(About* NATALYA*)* Look at her. Look who's talking, huh? Mistress of the house—ha! Vassa Petrovna! What kind of people do we have here? Everyone says Russians are soft, kind. Others say we're nasty.

NATALYA: Have you seen a nasty person here? We are not nasty at all.

LIUDMILA: *(To* ANNA*)* What do you think? Are we nasty?

ANNA: Whatever all of you are, I am the same.

PAVEL: *(To* ANNA*)* Oh, so you've seen the light, Anna. You know you're damned.

LIUDMILA: I refuse to believe that there are genuinely nasty people here.

PROKHOR: Your faith, Liuda. It's always amazed me!

LIUDMILA: There are only unhappy people is all I'm saying. And they are unhappy because they can't love anything.

PAVEL: I'm unhappy! And I love…me!

LIUDMILA: And no one knows what is "Good".

PAVEL: *(To* LIUDMILA*)* So what is "Good"?

MIKHAIL: Liuda, you don't need to say anything. In fact, don't.

LIUDMILA: Your garden is Good, Mother! I've loved it since I was a little girl and now when I walk there I love you because you created it.

VASSA: *(Proudly, to* ANNA*)* Did you hear? What a woman!

PAVEL: Get me a shovel. It's getting deep in here.

LIUDMILA: Sometimes I am afraid of you.

PAVEL: Oops! She's gone and stepped in it.

MIKHAIL: Liudmila!

VASSA: Leave her alone.

LIUDMILA: Don't worry, Daddy! *(Back to* VASSA*)*

I can look at the garden and remember you, bent over, weeding around the apple trees and berries and flowers. You know, Mama, what is "Good!" You know. But besides you, no one knows—

PROKHOR: Oh yes, Vassa Petrovna Zheleznova is the essence of Good. Better than Jesus? Yahweh?

SEMYON: Natalya—"je!"

NATALYA: But it's blasphemous, this talk.

LIUDMILA: No one knows and won't know. Ever! Everything else "Good" will pass by, perhaps on the next street. Everything.

PAVEL: What is she after? Liudmila, what are you doing?

SEMYON: Pavel, even I can see it. Anna and Liudmila— they're both sucking up to Mother. Because neither of them will inherit anything.

VASSA: You better keep your thoughts to yourself. Thinking is not for everybody, my boy!

NATALYA: He isn't afraid of anyone.

SEMYON: "Je!"

VASSA: What stupid word is that that you keep repeating?

SEMYON: "Je." It's simply— "je!"

VASSA: Oh, Semyon, Semyon!

PAVEL: Liuda, go on. Give us more. Surely you have another shovelfull.

LIUDMILA: I don't want to.

VASSA: And you don't need to. God bless you with healthy children, Liudmila.

LIUDMILA: *(About* PAVEL*)* With him? How can one have healthy children with him?

MIKHAIL: Oh, that tongue of yours.

PROKHOR: And we were having such a nice moment, too.

PAVEL: *(Takes a cup, heads for* LIUDMILA*)* I will kill you!

*(*VASSA *pushes him under his elbow and makes him drop the cup.* PAVEL *turns on his mother.)*

PAVEL: What are doing? Protecting her? Well, give me my share right now, my money! Give me my money and go to—

VASSA: *(Pushing him)* Shush!

PAVEL: *(Choked with words)* I hate you all. I will set a fire! I will—I will—do something! Who are you to me? *(Almost crying)* Mother…Are you really a mother? Uncle? Wife? Brother? *Sister?* Who are you?

ANNA: Pavel—

PAVEL: You hunt me like the dogs hunt a rabbit and what for? Give me mine and I will leave!

VASSA: But what is yours? What do you own?

NATALYA: How dare you! Everything is his and Senia's.

ANNA: Be quiet, Natalya!

NATALYA: Why should I?

VASSA: You were told to stop talking, you troublemaker!

NATALYA: *(Crying)* Senia! Why are they doing this to me!

PROKHOR: *(To ANNA)* I had better leave the room. I can't take this!

SEMYON: Are we still children? Everyone wants to live on their own.

PROKHOR: Where are my pills? I always keep them here.

ANNA: I'll go get them. *(She exits.)*

PROKHOR: No! Don't leave me! Get me out of here! Someone! Vassa! For god's sake!

*(VASSA doesn't move.)*

PROKHOR: Liudmila. Come here. Help me. Please.

VASSA: Liudmila, come here!

PROKHOR: Oh go! I am man enough to calm myself down. There. See? Vassa Petrovna? I don't need your help. Although it is clear that you've left me in the cage with the rabid beast. But I'm going to be fine. *(Another angina pain)* Where is Anna and my medicine!!

LIUDMILA: I'll get her!!

*(She starts to go but PAVEL grabs her by the arm and stops her.)*

PAVEL: What!? You want to help him? When he wronged me?!! You—you and him!!!

PROKHOR: Pavel, let go of her!

PAVEL: (*Screams*) I am Master here! Me, the freak! Let him die…and all of you with him!

(*Restraining her, he shoves* LIUDMILA *in front of* PROKHOR)

PAVEL: And you'll never get to lay a hand on her again! Because she's mine! MINE!

PROKHOR: (*Turning purple, getting up from his chair, hissing*) Youuuuu…I said let go of her!!!

(PAVEL *throws* LIUDMILA *towards* PROKHOR.)

PAVEL: (*In his face*) Right, I will…kill you! I will hit you in the face!!

(*Total turmoil.* SEMYON *screams and takes* PAVEL's *arm to keep him from hitting* PROKHOR. NATALYA *tries to get* PROKHOR *back in his chair.*)

NATALYA: Pasha, leave him alone.

LIUDMILA: (*To* MIKHAIL) Daddy, can't you do something?

PROKHOR: I need my medicine! Somebody help me.

VASSA: Stay there, Mikhail.

(PAVEL *starts to try to get free of* SEMYON's *grip:*)

SEMYON: Pashka—stop it! Uncle—get out of here! Mother!!

VASSA: Let Pavel go, Semyon. He's a grown man.

(SEMYON *lets* PAVEL *go and* PAVEL *attacks* PROKHOR.)

PAVEL: You made me do this!!

(PAVEL *punches* PROKHOR *in the chest.* PROKHOR *rises and kicks* PAVEL's *foot.* PAVEL, *moaning, drops on the floor.* PROKHOR *collapses back into his chair.*)

SEMYON: *(To* NATALYA*)* Let's get out of here quickly.

NATALYA: *(To* SEMYON*)* Wait a minute.

PAVEL: I'm in such pain! Can anyone help me?

*(*ANNA *enters.)*

ANNA: *(About* PROKHOR*)* I have his medicine. Give him some water.

MIKHAIL: *(To* LIUDMILA*)* Liudmila, come here.

VASSA: Liudmila, hot water.

LIUDMILA: But you're supposed to use cold water, aren't you?

MIKHAIL: Stay out of it.

ANNA: Yes, Mother—hot water onto his heart.

MIKHAIL: We should take him to his room.

LIUDMILA: But—should he be moved?

ANNA: *(Praising those who are helping to move* PROKHOR, *ignoring* LIUDMILA*)* Right. That's good. Let's take him to his room…Semyon, help us!

NATALYA: Don't touch him, Senia! I'm scared! They got Pavel going on purpose!

*(*MIKHAIL, ANNA, SEMYON *carry* PROKHOR *out)*

VASSA: Liudmila, stay there!

NATALYA: Senya, don't—Senya.

VASSA: *(To* NATALYA*)* You're hissing. Stop it.

*(They are gone with* PROKHOR. PAVEL *gets up and goes to* VASSA, *dragging his injured foot and holding on to the chairs for support.)*

NATALYA: What? Are you calling me a snake?

VASSA: What did you say?

NATALYA: You may not talk to me that way anymore, Mother-in-law.

VASSA: Why is that? What's changed, you cabbage?

NATALYA: What's changed, Mother-in-law, is we are not beholden to you anymore. We are masters here!

VASSA: Oh, get out!

(SEMYON *comes back in time to hear this.*)

NATALYA: *(About* VASSA*)* Senia, she screamed at me!

SEMYON: *(Trying to seem self-confident)* You, Mother, stop it! I am thirty-one. And Pasha is thirty-four! You can't dispute this fact.

(VASSA *just looks at him.*)

SEMYON: What are you staring at? Well, you can stare however much you want but there is the law of inheritance. Sons are heirs. Accordingly. There is no dispute about that either!

VASSA: *(To* PAVEL*)* Pavel, go to your room!

PAVEL: I don't want to. I won't go.

SEMYON: Well. Now it is up to us. It's going to be how we want things to be.

VASSA: You were born a fool, Semyon!

SEMYON: You'd better think twice about what you call me. I may be a "fool" but according to the law, I am the master now. And you, if you please—

ANNA: *(Enters)* Mother, I think Uncle Prokhor is dead.

(MIKHAIL *enters and nods to confirm that fact.* LIUDMILA *is the only one who shows any sign of grief. Silence.* NATALYA *crosses herself three times, but can barely hide her pleasure at his death.*)

SEMYON: My god…

PAVEL: He's dead?

NATALYA: *(Whispering to* SEMYON*)* Now—you'll have to inherit! Everything will be ours!

LIUDMILA: Oh, be quiet! He's gone. Barely a minute ago.

VASSA: Well, Pavel, I treated you like an adult. And the first thing you do is kill someone.

*(VASSA exits with MIKHAIL to go look at PROKHOR)*

PAVEL: Me! Me? But it's not my fault. It was just an argument! We've had hundreds of them! *(He looks at the hand he hit PROKHOR with.)* I'm drunk. Everyone can see I am drunk!

SEMYON: Pashka! Watch yourself!

PAVEL: *(Looks at ANNA)* Sister Anna. You wouldn't help me now if you could. I see you. I know all about you now.

NATALYA: Pasha! You can tell me—they got you going on purpose, didn't they. You all got him going and it's happened—

PAVEL: It's not my fault. I'm drunk. He's old.

*(VASSA and MIKHAIL enter.)*

VASSA: He's dead.
You know, we don't have a friendly family. People aren't our friends. And there will be some… unpleasant rumors.

PAVEL: I was drunk, Mother! It was an accident!

VASSA: There will be a police investigation. Because money is involved! Prokhor had a lot of money in the business.

PAVEL: Mama—

VASSA: And you, my son, you were told—don't touch him, you might kill him. Yet you, on purpose—

PAVEL: What was I supposed to do? He attacked me!! Mama? Senia?

NATALYA: Don't worry, Pashka, God knows who the guilty ones are.

VASSA: Good point, Natalya. You're right. Listen to your sister-in-law.

(NATALYA *is stunned by the compliment.* VASSA *turns on* PAVEL.)

VASSA: How are you going to justify yourself in front of God? If you are to ever resolve this sinful matter and have some peace ever in your life, you must take some strong action — you must go to a monastery.

LIUDMILA: The answer! Mother!

(LIUDMILA *crosses to* VASSA, *smiling all the way*)

PAVEL: I don't want to! What are you doing? Semyon, I don't want this!

VASSA: I have already made a big donation to the monastery through Father Yegor. How much was it I gave to Father Yegor?

(MIKHAIL *is trying to figure out what she means.*)

VASSA: When we paid him?

MIKHAIL: One thousand rubles.

PAVEL: You sold me for a thousand rubles? You sold me, your son, for a thousand rubles! And Liudmila, you're happy! Can you see what they're trying to do to me! How happy you are—I can see it in your face!

VASSA: (*To* PAVEL) Pavel, don't you see—nobody will be laughing at you there. Nobody will blame you for being ugly. And, most of all, no one will ask any difficult questions about Prokhor's death. You had a fight, he died, and you went into a monastery.

PAVEL: (*To* LIUDMILA) Smiling at my downfall? I will never forget it.

LIUDMILA: No, Pavel. I am smiling at my freedom.
You are a human being, after all! Do you have at least
a drop of kindness? For God's sake, let me go! I will
always speak well of you. I swear, I will think of you
with tenderness in my heart. But I can't be with you!
Even touching you hurts me...especially after you've
killed someone...Pavel! Pasha! My dear, let me go!

PAVEL: There is no need... Don't say any more. It
doesn't matter. Divorce or something. Well...I don't
care now.

(LIUDMILA *crosses to him and, being careful not to touch
him, kisses him on the forehead*)

PAVEL: What? Finally a kiss, as if I were dead? And
you, Mother, I am not going to a monastery, damn
you. Police and all that—you lie! You want to grab
my money, don't you! Give me my money and I will
leave...to the end of the world and away from all of
you! You will never hear of me again, never! Who
knows? I might get rich, and you—will be beggars, all
of you, and come to me for charity. And I will give an
order that you be driven away from my doorstep while
I watch out the window as you run away. Give me my
money! And then, you won't see me any more—ever!

VASSA: I won't give you any money, any of you.

NATALYA: Why not? You can't do this.

PAVEL: You give it to me!

SEMYON: But there is the law of inheritance, Mother.

VASSA: I heard that when you said it before, Semyon.
However, we have a legal document that—what is the
word, Mikhail?

MIKHAIL: (*As he goes to fetch the documents*)
"Supercedes."

VASSA: —yes, supercedes the law of inheritance.

MIKHAIL: *(As he passes one to* SEMYON *and one to* PAVEL*)*
These are copies. The original has been filed in town.

VASSA: Would one of you boys read it aloud, so we can
all hear?

SEMYON: *(Too devastated)* I can't.

*(*NATALYA *grabs it away from him.)*

NATALYA: I will. *(Reading)* "I, Zakhar Ivanovich
Zheleznova, leave all my assets, including house,
factory and earnings thereunto— *(She stops—she can't
go on—she's read ahead enough to know what it says To*
SEMYON*)* They forged it!

VASSA: *(Looking directly at* NATALYA *and finishing the
phrase)* "—to my wife, Vassa Petrovna Zheleznova, for
her sole, unrestricted ownership."

MIKHAIL: Witnessed by Father Yegor, who visited this
house almost daily while Zakhar was dying, by Antip
Stepanov Mukhoedov, well known to you. And by
Ryzhev, the landowner.

SEMYON: Mother, you can't do this to us!

PAVEL: *(Crumples up the will and throws it at* MIKHAIL*)*
It doesn't matter. I never believed in my freedom,
anyway. And now I know I don't get to be free. It's
simple now. I have to go to the monastery. I can't stay
here and I have no money to go anywhere else.

NATALYA: Can't we do anything? Senia?

*(*SEMYON *shakes his head "no".)*

PAVEL: Good-bye, Liudmila. Oh, you already said
good-bye. Well, kiss me once more, out of charity,
then. Will you?

LIUDMILA: *(Crosses to him)* All right, but keep your
hands away. Don't touch me.

PAVEL: Then never mind. Never mind all of you. You're all devils! And I'm leaving Hell at last!! *(He exits, running.)*

VASSA: *(To* MIKHAIL*)* Look after him! Hurry up.

MIKHAIL: I need to report Prokhor's death.

VASSA: Then do that!
No, see if Pavel is all right first.
Mischa—it's quite common for relatives to suffer heart attacks at the funerals of their loved ones.

MIKHAIL: Yes, Vassa Petrovna.

*(*MIKHAIL *exits.* VASSA *turns to* SEMYON.*)*

VASSA: Semyon, it's time for you to go, too. Across the river with your in laws. I'll run the business without you, Senechka. You never cared about it. Never.

SEMYON: I could try harder. I could—

VASSA: You're thirty-one years old, as you constantly remind me. It's time you learned to live without your mother.

NATALYA: No, Semyon, let me—
Forgive me, Mother-in-law, for whatever—

VASSA: And you—I definitely don't want to see you again. Now go!

*(*NATALYA *and* SEMYON *exit noiselessly, devastated.* VASSA *staggers a bit.)*

ANNA: *(Helping her to keep her balance)* What's wrong? Mother!

VASSA: I don't feel well.
Get me some water—cold.

*(*LIUDMILA *runs out to get the water)*

ANNA: You are exhausted.

VASSA: Don't tell me how I feel. *(Beat)* You took a long time to get Prokhor's medicine.

ANNA: It was hard to find.

VASSA: And what happened upstairs? When you got Prokhor back to his room? The last time.

ANNA: Survival, Mother.

*(Beat)*

LIUDMILA: *(Running in with the water, gives it to VASSA)* The monastery idea—that is so brilliant. How did you come up with that on the spot? It's a miracle.

VASSA: On the spot? I have been thinking about it for years—where to put him. Hundreds of nights I haven't slept. There was no miracle. They don't exist! We must do everything for ourselves.

LIUDMILA: Good heavens, someone is dead upstairs, someone I knew. And I don't feel anything!

VASSA: *(Quietly)* Are you happy?

LIUDMILA: I can start over.

VASSA: Stay with me. You can get married again…Give birth to children… You can live with Anna and me and her children. *(She listens for something she thinks she hears.)* Children will be running everywhere—a new start. What? What is that sound?

ANNA: I can't hear anything, Mama.

VASSA: Nothing? I swear I heard…
So my sons are worthless. So what, I pity them. One has his wife's family. They'll be good for him. But my other son, my first born… *(Gets up, worried)* Someone is screaming. Do I hear screaming?

LIUDMILA: No. No one. Are you all right?

VASSA: It's Pavel—

LIUDMILA: No one, Mother. It's silent. At last.

VASSA: In the garden.

LIUDMILA: *(To* VASSA*)* No one's anywhere.

ANNA: *(To* VASSA*)* No one's in the garden. Everything is fine now. It's over.

VASSA: *(To* ANNA*)* Don't use that tone with me. I am still your mother.

*(*LIUDMILA *and* ANNA *go to her to try to comfort her. She waves them away.)*

VASSA: And I am fine. But I will never have a moment's peace—never!

## END OF PLAY